K

with A. Rochester

The Backside of the Story:
*My Personal Journey into the
Black Market Butt Injection
Scandal*

"A story told so well; I had no idea I would clearly understand the enormous struggle one would go through to look a certain way."

—Tamika Newhouse, Author and Publisher

(Paperback)

ISBN-13: 978-0-692-22465-6

ISBN-10: 0692224653

Cover design by Davida Baldwin of OBD (Odd Ball Design)

First Edition August 2014

Dedication

For all of my clients, you deserve to know the truth.

TABLE OF CONTENTS

TABLE OF CONTENTS (continued)

TABLE OF CONTENTS (continued)

Foreword

I met Kimberly Smedley shortly before she was to go to prison for illegally injecting silicone into hundreds of women's behinds. This 21st century phenomenon surprised many, and folks couldn't understand why. Why were women getting their butts maxi enhanced, and why are men so drawn to huge behinds? Well, if you think about it, it's always been an attraction, even for white men. Just take a look at the upper class women of the 1800s who wore corsets and bustles under fine dresses to make the waist smaller and the behind look much larger as she strolled past and attracted that 19th century man.

I was impressed with Kimberly's calmness as she knew she had to face the unknown—jail. But she's come out incredibly strong with a big and smart tale to tell about round and huge 21st century tail.

Jamie Foster Brown, Editor
Sister 2 Sister Magazine

Acknowledgments

Simply put, "GOD IS AMAZING!"

Everybody that knows me, knows that one of my favorite quotes is "TEAM WORK MAKES THE DREAM WORK." Well, here's to my DREAM TEAM:

Tiffany Gregory (TipTop), I remember laughing at you when you told me all the good things I could and would be. I didn't know you were really speaking into my life. I love you so.

Gieava Stinchcomb (Gigi), what can I say besides you are the bomb! Keep on going, girl. I can't thank you enough. You are always there. You may be late, but always on time to save the day. Muah! I love you so.

Tamika Newhouse, who would have thought that we would be here, now. Wow! What started out as drinks and talk about kids, turned into a wonderful thing. Thank you. I love you so.

Linda Wilson, the best editor ever. You took something that was good and made it GREAT. Thanks, I love you so.

My "Jeanie Weenie," thanks for raising an independent, strong woman. I love you so, Mama.

Norma Jones (Diamond), I can never take back what you endured with me. Take your arms and hug yourself tight. That's how much you mean to me, my sister. Thanks for hanging in there. Muah! I love you so.

Kobie Jones, the best nephew ever. Thanks for the encouragement. I love you so.

Charles Harris (my big Poppa), you have a heart of gold. You love me unconditionally. You stand on the sidelines and cheer me on. Thank you. I love you so.

Al Janae Williams, thank you so much for putting together the initial meeting between Tamika and me. Look at what you started. I love you so.

My kids (Daton, Brandon, and Lil Ms. Kareema), I truly am thankful for you guys. It's because of you that my life is grounded. No matter the age, you will always be my babies. You make it easy to keep going. I love you so much.

Veronica Adadevoh, I thank you for every positive word you've spoken into my life. They still linger in the atmosphere. I love you so.

The Browns (Eric and Erika), you were there through the tears and the heartache and all the pain I've endured that led up to this. I couldn't ask for a better brother/friend and sister/friend. Thanks for having my back and my front. I love you so.

My three special girls (Kari, Kaylin, and Lil Ms. Taylor), hey my girls. I appreciate you so. Thanks for never judging me. Be happy and LIVE! I love you so.

Ambra Horton, thank you for being there when I needed you. You never hesitated. I love you so.

Carl Sneed (Kia), you have kept me laughing for the past five years, and I look forward to many more. I'm glad we adopted each other. Boy, ain't we dysfunctional? But hey, I love you so.

Robert, I can't wait for us to travel and live it up again. Next time it's on me. I love you so.

To Austin Roberts, thank you for being in my life. You were sent on special assignment and didn't even know it. We shared some good times and some sad times, however, I choose to remember the good. I miss you as if you left yesterday, but we will always be connected. Thank you. I love you so.

Kurby and Melissa, the "Dynamic Duo." Thanks, cousins, for the love and never ending support. I love you so.

Nakia Roberson, when I told you about this project you didn't ask any questions. You stepped right in. You are truly a godsend. Thank you. I love you so.

Jody "Jo Jo" Kurtz, thank you from the bottom of my heart. I love you so.

The McKinneys, there is so much to be said because there is so much history there. I can't say one thing about one without saying something about the other. From the grandmom on down to the grandkids. But here goes: Thank you. I LOVE YOU ALL SO.

Naz (my brother), thanks for always lending me an ear. You motivated me on many occasions. Just know you are truly missed. I love you so.

Virginia McDonald, you know how to unclutter my world and keep the energy around me clean. LOL. I love you so.

Joe Robinson, we've had our ups and downs and we're still standing. I appreciate you. Muah! I love you so.

Atarah McQuinn, we walked many days on that track, and I will never forget you. Some days if it weren't for you I would have lost it. Thanks friend/sis. I love you so.

Hey Electric Shop (Mack, Rochelle, Ebony, KeKe, Vee Vee (HRIC), Tremaine). We had some fun times, didn't we? I'm glad it's over. I love you all so.

Donna Roy (DK from the VA), how could I forget you? I love you so.

Latronne, Kenyetta, and Tiffany, thank you ladies for covering for me while I put this project together. You all can breathe easy now. I love you so.

Aisha Hall, you are awesome and have the sweetest disposition. Thank you for working with me on this project. Your talent is amazing! I love and appreciate you so.

Eugenia Johnson (Vee), thanks for being there in my time of need. It didn't go unnoticed. I love you so.

Attorney Steven Berne, the best attorney ever! Thanks for your loyalty and hard work. I love you so.

Kendrick Harris, thanks for believing in me. I love you so.

BTW, if I left anybody out, please charge it to my head and not my heart. I had to leave pages to tell my story. LOL.

By now, readers, I know you are probably saying, "She loves everybody." But guess what? I DO! Thank you all for your support.

To all the book clubs and book stores, much gratitude.

Remember, "Our DREAMS should always be bigger than us."

Enjoy.

K

Prologue

The Bed I Made

I couldn't believe I was standing in a United States Federal Courtroom in Baltimore, Maryland awaiting my sentence. All for helping women feel better about themselves. Didn't the judge understand how many lives I had changed for the better? Before this situation, my life was in order. I had it all together . . . or so I thought. It seemed like just yesterday I was at the top of my game, making great money, traveling spending time with my family, and I even had a new love. Then all at once my life spiraled out of control. How did I let this happen? Yes, I had told God I was tired and needed a change in my life. But come on, God! This wasn't anything close to what I had in mind. People have often said, "Be careful what you ask for."

While facing the judge, I turned to look back at my family. My mom sat in the first row crying silently. I knew she was hurt and afraid. Seeing her cry almost caused me to break down. With me being her only child, the possibility that I might leave her was too much to bear. Most of my family sat in the courtroom, teary-eyed. They always thought so highly of me. I wondered, *"What would they think of me now?* My cousin Tracy sat there consoling my mom, trying to be strong. She was as close to a sibling as I had. I felt so bad for her. Because of this case, Tracy nearly lost her job as a flight attendant. Twenty-one years of employment almost discarded because the Feds tried to bring her into my drama. My cousin, who has never had more than a speeding ticket, was accused of using her employment to help me commit my crime. Thank God after much fighting she was able to prove them wrong. Yet, here she was standing by me. Her son sat beside her looking solemn. When I looked at him, he smiled. That was just like Cody, always trying to uplift his "Auntie Kim."

My daughter, Keron, held her head down, scratching her arm. My poor child. The drama surrounding my arrest and trial caused her a great deal of anxiety at the precious age of ten. She was in therapy because she began self-inflicting. This entire ordeal had taken a toll on her and was too much to deal with at such a young age. My oldest son, Dave, sat there stone-faced, trying to hold it together and be courageous. I was so proud of him. He had turned out to be a fine young man. I knew he was torn up by this situation. My home girl, Kelly, kept a straight face. It was difficult to figure out what she was thinking. I can tell you this: she couldn't stand the Feds and knew firsthand how ruthless they could be. So I appreciated her being here, and until then I didn't realize how much I needed their support. At that moment, I wished I could do everything all over.

My thoughts were interrupted by the judge's firm voice. "Ms. Smedley," she said, "though no individuals have come forward to testify against you, we are still unsure of the long term health risks associated with your crime. Because these risks are unknown, your sentence is . . ." Everything around me began to go in slow motion.

The US Attorney had asked for a sentence not less than forty-two months and a $250,000 fine. Judges weren't bound by any request, not even a plea agreement. So she could go above or below the guidelines. Just because I had accepted a plea agreement didn't guarantee anything. So I had no idea what was about to happen.

Yes, I knew what I was doing was against the law, but I never thought it would be me, Kimberly Smedley, up against the United States Government. I thought if I ever got caught up, it would be a state case. But I was sadly mistaken. Nothing, and I do mean *nothing*, could have prepared me for this.

"Your sentence is 36 months imprisonment and a $25,000 fine. You've been doing this for quite some time, Ms. Smedley." The judge continued her legal jargon, but I didn't hear any of it. Numb . . . I did, however, feel a sense of relief that the judge chose not to go along with the US Attorney's recommendation.

Still, prison was prison, and time was time. Any extended period away from my children and family was going to be difficult.

My life had gone from sugar to shit in a matter of months. The sentence really was a disappointment, but it didn't shock me. My attorney, Steven Berne, had already told me the US Attorney was asking for some prison time. My attorney asked for a year and a day and no fine. I wasn't surprised about the prison time; I just thought it would be less than thirty-six months.

What shocked me more than anything and blew my mind was the man I loved and respected a great deal had come into the courtroom and actually testified against me. Yes, he crossed the ultimate line.

Now, let's not get it twisted, I loved Marvin, but I wasn't *in love* with him. For reasons known and unknown, I held the deepest parts of my love back from him. When I would debate with myself about going to the next level with Marvin, something inside me told me, "Don't do it." I guess my soul had sensed something wasn't right—as if the spirit of betrayal or foul play dwelled within him. If we listen to our intuition it never fails us.

Marvin and I traveled together almost weekly, and sometimes twice a week. He wasn't only my lover and friend; he did security for me when I was working. When I wasn't working, we traveled together every six to eight weeks to the Caribbean. We both loved the islands and had genuine fun. I thought we were building something. I exposed him to things he'd never seen, to foods he'd never tasted, and took him to places he'd never been. *Really Marvin! What kind of person turns on you in such a cowardly way?*

What upset me most was that I took a plea, accepting responsibility for things I never would have, had I known Marvin was the government's only witness. I expected it to be someone whom I had beef with, or a competitor to do something like this, but never Marvin. He was their entire case.

Yeah, the lead agent had contacted some of my clients, but none would testify against me. Many even called me during the investigation to let me know they had been contacted. They told me they didn't say anything, but I wasn't sure at the time. But now I know they really didn't. My clients were more loyal than the man I shared my deep secrets with.

I was attracted to Marvin in a different way than I had been attracted to other men. Kanye said it best: "Now I ain't saying she a gold digger, but she ain't messin' wit' no broke . . . You know the rest. I was used to men who had no problem supporting me financially. But Marvin . . . let's just say I let a few things slide. He never had a lot of money, but I was attracted to him because he seemed to appreciate the finer things in life, even though he couldn't afford them. What he lacked in the finance department, he definitely made up for in the romance department. So many men forget about chivalry, and oftentimes we forget to demand it, but I didn't have to remind Marvin. It was automatic. He was debonair and knew how to treat a lady. I remember we attended my god sister's wedding in Las Vegas. A few women had come unaccompanied, and he showed them such a good time by catering to them. By the end of the trip they were teasing me, asking when we were breaking up so they could have him, including my god sister's mom. I knew they were joking, but with him it wasn't a front. That part of him is truly who he is and that's what I loved.

Marvin and I had the type of relationship you read about in a love story or see in an old black and white romantic movie. We would stroll down the streets of DC, NY, or wherever we were that week, holding hands and gazing at one another. Marvin never let me walk on the outside of the sidewalk. I thought he'd be my protector. He was the first man to order my meals from the menu for me. For those ladies who have a man with these old school qualities, you know what I'm talking about. His nobility left me awestruck because I typically dated street guys all my life. I had a thing for hustlers and I don't know why. Yeah, they would keep my pockets full of cash, but there was nothing like quality romance, chivalry, and a man knowing how to be a man. Which is why I still couldn't believe Marvin was offering up his testimony against me.

When my attorney informed me just two days before my sentencing what was going to happen, I immediately felt sick. The conversation as I can recall, went something like this:

"Hey Kim, this is Steven."

"Hey Steven," I replied.

Every time he called, my eyes instantly darted toward my mini bar. I had to calm my nerves after every conversation. Especially now, since sentencing was around the corner.

"You doing okay?" he asked.

"Yes, Steven," I replied, hoping he'd cut the small talk and get to it. Small talk with Steven was a dead give-away that some bad news was lurking nearby.

"Well, I have some good news and some bad news," he said. Steven just didn't understand how much I *hated* when he would say things like that to me.

"I knew it," was all I could get my mouth to speak.

"The good news is that there aren't any other people who will be testifying. That's a good thing because the Feds can play dirty."

"So, what's the bad news?" I asked.

By this time I had made my way over to the bar, ready to take a long swig of Johnnie Walker Blue Label straight from the bottle. What bad news could there actually be? What could be worse than what was already happening? There were no cooperators and that was great. When dealing with the Feds, cooperation is everything. In other words, snitches usually make their cases for them. A lot of times, they may not even have a case, but with the Feds, hearsay is admissible, and all they need is someone to testify against you. Many times, they don't even need any evidence.

"The bad news is," my lawyer went on to say, "that someone *is* going to say some things, and he's their only witness. But he's going to be damaging since it's at your sentencing."

"Who is it?" I asked.

My lawyer referenced the word "he," so it must've been one of my male competitors hating on me. But then again, who knows. All I knew was that I was too mentally exhausted to even try and figure it out.

"It's Marvin Freemont. Your boyfriend!"

Saying I felt sick is an understatement. The betrayal and hurt was so intense, I thought I would pass out. *How could he*? This man lay in my bed and told me how much he loved me. I spent time with his children. We were . . . well, Marvin and Kim. The nausea hit me when I thought about the plea deal I signed. I didn't think there was anyone speaking against me. This shocked the hell out of a sista. I signed a plea admitting to things and accepting responsibility for things that I didn't have to, only to protect my closest friends, family, and some of my clients. Had I known the only evidence they had against me was Marvin, I wouldn't have signed the plea agreement. Damn you Marvin!

So many scenarios began to flood my mind. Did Marvin set me up from the beginning? Was he working for the Feds? I wondered if it was me. Had I done something to make him angry? We were not supposed to be on opposite sides of the fence. I guess you really don't know a person like you think you do. I shared so much with him about my life, and I let him see into my secret world and he exposed me.

The day of my sentencing hearing was such an emotional disaster. I sat in the courtroom and tried my hardest not to even look at him. All I kept thinking was, *How could he*? Everybody has heard stories of girlfriends testifying against boyfriends and such, but this was happening to *me*. To experience it firsthand was so much more different than sympathizing with someone. Talk about sleeping with the enemy.

When he walked into the courtroom, I noticed some physical changes in him. It seemed as if he started to gray in his beard overnight. He was forty-eight years old, but now he looked much older. This was such a sudden change, far from the natural, slight graying that I was accustomed to. No, uh-uhn, this was the result of stress, but there were many possibilities for the stress.

For one, Marvin was already an outcast. He was an ex-DC police officer. The reason he lost his job was because he snitched, blew the whistle, let the cat out of the bag. Call it whatever you want, but he told about some shady dealings regarding the department and had been an outcast ever since.

Second, Marvin had a woman he was living with. His story was that she was holding him down since he'd lost his job as a police officer. A man who must depend on a woman for his well-being can easily feel a great deal of pressure being placed on his ego and pride.

Our relationship was based on work and good times, so I wasn't tripping about his living situation. Plus, I wasn't taking care of any man. I was taught better than that. So I was fine with his woman doing the things I wouldn't do. She could keep the headaches; I just wanted to enjoy the perks. I already had a man that I was in love with, but I still missed Marvin. So with all of that thrown in the mix, it could have been anything stressing him. Remember, I said I made some exceptions for him.

I hadn't seen Marvin since my arrest back in September 2011. It was now July 2012. Marvin still had swag. Always a confident man, he possessed an arrogance that I loved. When we were out together and men would try to flirt with me, it didn't bother him the least bit. He loved to see other men show me attention. That motivated him to pull me close, throwing the fact that I belonged to him in any of my admirers' faces. He was only about five-feet-nine, but he stood as if he were six-feet-five. I loved that about him.

During my extended view of Marvin, something struck me as odd. He wore a taqiyah on his head. Yeah, I knew his religion was Hebrewism, but he'd never worn that thing on his head before. Yet, he chose today to do so. Humph! Fool me twice, why don't you! Marvin walked toward the witness stand, keeping his focus where he knew he was to stand. He didn't bother to look my way. I was more broken at that moment than at any I could think of.

"Raise your right hand," the bailiff called out.

"It is against my religion to swear on a Bible. I would rather not," Marvin said, cuffing his hands before himself and pressing them up against his chest.

The bailiff nodded and said, "Do you swear to tell the whole truth and nothing but the truth?"

Marvin said, "That's what I'm here for."

The bailiff said, "Sir, answer the question. Yes or no?"

I was annoyed already, and Marvin hadn't even started his testimony. I rolled my eyes. *He can't even answer the questions. He talks too damn much. Just say yes or no. Damn!"*

My lawyer, Steven Berne, leaned toward me and whispered, "I had no clue Marvin was Muslim."

I rolled my eyes and laughed. "Apparently, neither did he," I whispered back. *Is this the same man that was so anti-white this and anti-white that, sitting here on the stand telling all of my business? Our business!*

Once upon a time we were Bonnie and Clyde. Marvin had worked in law enforcement for twenty years. He spoke of how corrupt the laws were and had often complained about his job. Maybe too much.

The US Attorney on my case stood up and walked toward Marvin and said, "State your name."

"Marvin Freemont."

As he began to speak, I just closed my eyes and fought tooth and nail to keep the tears from falling. But let me tell you, those tears were fighting back, trying to break free. It was a battle. So I used the only weapon I had left, my memories, and summoned all the good times to the front of my brain and focused on them.

I thought about Marvin's oldest son, Kyle, traveling with my family and me to the West Indies. He bonded so well with my sons while we were on vacation, I felt as if he were a part of my family. With all my might I focused hard on the Marvin I once knew and not this stranger in court today. I had to do that; otherwise, I might have attacked him right in the courtroom, getting a whole new charge. He just wasn't worth it.

About two months before my sentencing, Marvin disappeared. I tried calling him on several occasions, but he wouldn't answer his phone. I figured he knew how stressed I was and didn't want to see me upset as I prepared for the worst. Silly me! I guess I couldn't have been more wrong. Marvin went missing because the prosecutor's threat of the worst possible sentence had sucked him in: probation. That's right, probation. Marvin turned informant because he couldn't handle probation. Unbeknownst to me at the time, Marvin had been subpoenaed by the grand jury. He actually perjured himself by telling them he didn't know anything about any injections. Of course, they found out that it was a lie. So they had him. You know the Feds: "Divide and Conquer."

While giving his testimony, he couldn't even look my way. Our three-year relationship meant absolutely nothing. At that moment I let it all go. It was what it was. I strongly believe in the prayer of "Serenity," and I knew that God had a plan for me. But right now, the bed I made, I had to lie in it.

Chapter 1

The Full Story

I'd seen enough butts in the last six hours to last me not one, but several lifetimes. I couldn't believe I had already done fifteen clients today, and I still had one more client to do before I called it a night.

This short, stout woman walked into the room with a nervous, anxious look in her huge brown eyes. I'd seen that look so many times, but didn't have the energy to encourage her like I usually did with new clients. I was ready to get it over with, so I snapped on my latex gloves and filled my syringe.

This was going to be a job. Her butt was seriously square shaped and flat, but she wanted a full, round booty. She wanted me to perform a miracle, but then again that's what I was good at doing. This was an art just as much as it was anything else.

She lay across the table and I—

Wait a minute! I'm moving too fast here. Before I get into the butt shots, let me give you the full story—my story . . .

Did you know mirrors play an important role in every female's life, both young and old the same? It's usually essential for many of us to look in it, but for some of us the mirror is a significant place to avoid. My image was always important, and it started when I was a little girl.

I was born on April 25, 1966, in Atlanta, Georgia, a pudgy little baby with a cute round face. My mom had me at the early age of eighteen. When I think back to my first memory of pretty, my mother immediately pops into my mind. She's a pretty lady, with distinctively white teeth and a beautiful smile. Her smile was literally perfect then, and still is now.

By the age of nine, almost every tooth in my mouth had a filling. I swore when I got older I would fix the problem, because image was important to me. If there was an issue with anything I saw in that mirror's reflection, it was getting fixed. Today I have spent a lot of money to make sure my teeth are beautiful. When you're a young child, the people around you make such an impression on you. Our concepts of beauty get imprinted into our minds early on, along with many other concepts of what we consider normal or abnormal.

My mom was tall and slender when she was young. My father, well, I remember very little about him. A very distinct memory I'll always have is his funeral. I had so many mixed emotions that day. Too much for a four-year-old mind to handle. *"God . . . How could you take my daddy away from me?"* I remember thinking over and over again.

I don't know what it is about daddies that make little girls crave them. Even if they don't know their father. I didn't even have a memory of how my daddy looked, or of ever spending any time with him, probably because I didn't. I could only recall his face from pictures.

While my mom was pregnant with me, she and my father broke up. She married a man named Napoleon Smedley. That's how I got Smedley as a last name. Mom told me she never loved him, but wanted to make sure that her baby had a place to call home.

That decision ended up being a bad one. This man abused my mom both physically and mentally. By the age of three, I went to live with my grandparents, Mama Essie and Uncle Willie. That's what I called them. Mama Essie had a butt so big I just knew I could sit a cup on it. It was big and round, like two cantaloupes stuffed into her pants. Mama Essie had a serious booty, and Uncle

Willie loved it. He was a short, stocky man who was very kind and soft-spoken. He never raised his voice about anything and reminded me of a bald Santa Claus. He chewed tobacco and Mama Essie dipped snuff, a finely-ground form of tobacco. She would pack her bottom lip with it.

Uncle Willie and Mama Essie couldn't have any children of their own, and my mom was of no blood relation to them. Nevertheless, they raised her from childhood. My biological grandmother, Mary, had given up all five of her children. That old African proverb, "It takes a village to raise a child" remained true. In those days you didn't need all kinds of paperwork and permission from the state to raise other people's kids. If you saw a child in need, you just took them in and made them your own. And that was that. I thank God for Mama Essie and Uncle Willie. My biological grandmother struggled with alcoholism, and my biological grandfather wasn't around. I didn't meet my biological grandfather until I was twelve. My mom always said she commended her mom for being strong enough to give her kids up. How many kids have to suffer because a parent is addicted to drugs and can't raise or provide for them properly? At least she knew she needed help. I believe that's why my mom always had a relationship with her until she passed away. She respected her for making a responsible and unselfish decision. Knowing all these things helped mold me into the selfless woman I am today.

I remember Mama Essie working for this white family. She would bring their laundry home, iron it, and take it back the next day. I used to sit and watch her perfectly iron underwear and sheets. She would tell me, "Kim, when you grow up, things gonna be different. You gonna have a good job. Dr. King changing some things. But if you don't find a good job, you find you a good white

3

family to work for." She was saying all of this while standing on her feet for several hours, ironing.

Although I was young, I thought, *I ain't never gone work for no white family.* But I knew better than to say it out loud because she would get on me for talking back. So I just said, "Yes, Mama." Mama Essie and my mom instilled a good work ethic in me, and I knew that working hard was a part of life.

During those times, many black women worked in the homes of white families, especially in the South. I would often hear stories of some of the wives going off on their white husbands for staring at that "nigger's butt." Many black women had these large fannies. Science today has shown that men tend to look at women with large rear ends and wide hips because they are hardwired for it. The reason being, larger hips signify good breeding.[1] It's an innate attraction, and wide hips just happen to be one of the features that get men's hormones jumping without them having to really think about it.

At the age of thirteen, I can remember distinctly checking the mirror to see how my butt looked. It hadn't come in yet. I was just a little girl, and as they say, my "hips hadn't spread yet." But I was a brown girl, and aren't we all supposed to be shapely? I patiently waited so that I too, could one-day sass around the house with a booty like Mama Essie's.

Back then I was proud of how I looked, and I was just as proud of how I imagined I was going to look when I got older. I just never thought that as a young girl, my self-love and image would be tested as drastically as it was.

All the older kids used to spoil me because I was the baby. One time I went to the neighborhood park to play, so I could run around for a few hours. I loved the playground because I could take off my shoes and play in the sand. Somehow, I got a bunch of sand in my hair. My mom didn't play that and having a messy head was a no-no. She kept my hair in neatly styled pigtails, and I had to be mindful of how I played. My older cousins were having a fit, fussing at me while trying to get the sand out of my hair. They knew if my mama saw it, there would be big trouble.

But then, something bizarre started to happen. A few days after the sand incident, I started to develop these weird sores all over my scalp. My mom began to panic and wanted to take me to a specialist to find out what in God's name was going on with her child's scalp.

Unfortunately, we didn't have a lot of money, so a specialist was out of the question. But we had to do something because it was getting worse.

Mom took me to the county hospital. People like us had to use the emergency room at the county hospital as our primary health care provider. The doctor examined my scalp and then told my mom the horrible diagnosis.

"Well, doctor, what's going on?" Mom asked.

"Your daughter has developed Infantigo. It's a condition you get when you have come into contact with, or have been around a dog with rabies." My mom assured the doctor that I hadn't been around any animals.

"We are going to have to shave all of her hair off."

And that's exactly what they did. I thought my mother was going to have a heart attack. My thick, strong, black pigtails were no more.

Mom acted as if it were her head being shaved. She was crying so hard I thought the nurse was gonna have to carry her out of the room. I felt sadder for her than I did for myself because Mom was so distraught. To be honest, it didn't bother me emotionally as much as it did physically. Every night my mom had to use a specially medicated shampoo on my head. She would pick off each scab in order to make sure the medication penetrated my scalp properly. Now that hurt! I cried from the pain and my mama would cry too. Sometimes she couldn't stand to do it, and her best friend Barbara would have to take over. It was just awful. To this present day, my scalp is still very sensitive.

One day my hair just started to grow back. No more painful sores or picking. Thank God! The year was 1971, and I was a proud girl, but even prouder about my new afro. Honey, I rocked my hair and didn't think nothing of it. I even likened myself as the female version of my favorite idol at the time, Michael Jackson. I just knew I was doing the darn thing, rocking bellbottom pants I begged my mom and grandmother to buy me. I wore a little leather vest with the shingles and I'd shimmy around. Nobody could tell me anything. Especially when I saw people on Soul Train boogying on down the Soul Train Line with their hair looking just like mine. I was okay with losing my pigtails. I figured this was the look God wanted me to have.

My mom was a completely different story though. She was walking around with my pigtails in a plastic bag showing everybody. Oh yes, she was definitely traumatized. Devastated even . . . I didn't understand why at that time. I thought I looked good. But then, my mom's reaction began to affect me. I thought, *Maybe something is wrong with the way I look. If there wasn't, she wouldn't be so upset.* I felt like I was making a mistake by being proud of my new hairdo. That was the first time an outside opinion about how I looked made me question something that I was originally okay with. Incidents where other people's opinions influenced my self-esteem would only get more intense as I grew older.

The Backside of the Story

There is nothing like feeling as though you don't fit in, or like you're ugly and something may be wrong with you. Other people can make you feel like that if you don't have high self-esteem. Kids can be ruthless, and if you aren't strong-minded, that type of harsh judgment can break you down.

We can't stop people from saying whatever it is they want to say, in whatever tone they choose to deliver it. But only one opinion matters and that is our own. Of course, everyone is entitled to his/her opinion, and we can't control or change that fact. What we can control is the power we give their opinions over our lives. We can debunk their insults and critiques by use of impeccable self-esteem. Self-esteem wasn't discussed with me or taught to me as a young woman. I now know instilling that into a child at a very young age is one of the greatest gifts you can give them. I only wish someone had taken the time to do that with me.

Chapter 2

Here Comes the Queen

I always knew that I loved making people look good, or as I liked to call it, 'enhancing their sexy.' I had been doing hair for about two years after getting my cosmetology license, and I was working at a hair salon in Downtown Atlanta in 1996.

The hair salon scene can be very busy. I met several clients and witnessed many stylists come and go. But I had become particularly close with a guy named Eric, who also worked at the salon. He kept me laughing and we talked about everything. Anyone who sat in his chair was transformed. He worked those fingers like the magician he was.

I liked many things about Eric, but what I liked most was his business mentality. He flipped houses on the side and made good extra money doing it. He would buy either a foreclosure or a fixer upper, renovate it, and then sell it. In Atlanta, the market had gotten so bad there seemed to be an endless supply of properties. Eric always tried to encourage me to spread my wings and lay a strong financial foundation for my children and me. I knew he was right, but I just didn't have the sense of urgency to make it happen at that time.

Back then I was making decent money doing hair, and I was also still with my son's father, who gave me plenty of extra money. I could just spend, spend, spend, chile, with no issues or worries. He was a hustler, so the money came fast. I spent it just as fast as he put it in my hands.

Sometimes he came into the salon and dropped off a few stacks. I'd stuff the money into my apron and start thinking about how quickly I needed to finish up my client so I could take my butt to Lenox Mall. I'd be smiling, humming, and flat ironing all at the same time. One day after I got some money from my son's father, I had that 'I'm about to spend, spend, spend' look on my face. Eric called me out.

"What?" I said to Eric after I noticed him shaking his head at me through the mirror.

"You know what, Ms. Thang? You just don't listen."

"Boy, what are you talking about?" I asked in a nonchalant way.

"Quick money goes quick! You need to do something with that money, girl. Your pockets are like an incinerator. You blow money like it grows on a tree." I laughed.

"You're right, Eric, and I'm going to get on top of things."

"Umm hmm. Okay! You better get in this housing game while it's hot," he warned. Eric was always trying to encourage me, and everybody needed a little motivation. I don't care what people say, gay friends to me, are the best friends.

On a busy day at the salon, a friend of Eric's named Lonzi walked into the shop. From the moment I laid eyes on Lonzi, I automatically fell in love with him. Honey, let me tell you there ain't nobody on this planet like Lonzi. I loved his personality from day one.

Lonzi owned a shop of his own on the other side of Atlanta, and like Eric, he was gay. But not just any gay; Lonzi was a Queen and he put the 'Q' in queen. He was a "flaming" queen! It was impossible not to notice him. His hair was cut in an asymmetrical bob and fell over his right eye. Bay-bee, you couldn't tell him his hair wasn't the bomb. He had cosmetic surgery done on his eyes, giving them that cat-like slant. He'd done his nose and even his chin. He reminded me of a mini Michael Jackson before he went overboard with his surgery.

If you wanted to avoid getting your feelings hurt, you didn't ever tell Lonzi he looked like Michael Jackson, because he would quickly tell you off.

"No sweetie, it's Prince whom I look like, so don't get it twisted." You just had to love Lonzi. And talk about a dresser, Lonzi could get as fly as a dapper don, honey. He liked to wear bright, colorful shirts to make sure you saw him coming from a mile away.

His favorite designer was Versace. He'd rock a Versace shirt, Versace shades, Versace belt and shoes. Oh, and we can't forget about his handbags. First of all, they were always big. The bigger, the better. They were expensive too. He only wore the best, Gucci, Louis Vuitton, Prada, Chanel, you name it, and he carried it on his arm. I didn't even know anything about Hermès until I met Lonzi, who was always dressed to the nines. Even his contact lenses matched the color of his shirts.

"Lonzi, why do your bags have to be so big?" I remembered asking him. He would snap that neck around and say, "Miss Kim, baby, when you have big money it is an absolute must that you have big bags!" I just shook my head, because no matter what I said to him, he had a quick response, usually sarcastic.

I am still trying to figure out how he managed to speak in this high-pitched female octave (think soprano) in an attempt to sound like a lady. Occasionally he got mad, and if you caught him in one of his 'going off' spells, that deep, manly voice would come roaring through. When he caught himself, he'd clear his throat, gather his thoughts, and go back into the female zone. He'd stand up straight, poke out his chest, and resume his position as the self-proclaimed Queen on a throne. I loved every minute of it!

He stood about 5-feet 10-inches tall and was very slim. His waist was about a size thirty-three. If anybody called him skinny, he quickly checked them. Also, he had a round butt because he had injections.

"You better smell it, baby, 'cause I ain't skinny. I am cute in the face and small in the waist," he would say, giving a quick runway model spin. "So don't hate!"

Everybody knew when Lonzi was coming into the shop. He made it a point to make sure you saw him. He drove a Mercedes Coupe that never saw the parking lot. He double parked right out front to ensure all spectators got a clear view of him about to make his grand entrance. When his car pulled up, stylists and clients and whoever else was around would all say in unison, "Here comes the Queen," and then crack up. Even the clients knew Lonzi.

That was all the motivation he needed to cut up. He'd sashay around the salon, and anyone who gave him a look he didn't like, he'd tell them, "Smell it, baby. Smell it!" That was his way of telling them "you know what it is." Lonzi was too funny. The entire shop would laugh at Lonzi acting a fool.

If someone had told me Lonzi was going to be one of the most important people in my life I would have laughed. I had no idea of the path Lonzi and I would soon embark on.

Honey, he came into the shop every week with some kind of drama. If you were down or having a bad day, Lonzi could make you forget about your problems. Your mouth, throat, and cheeks would be sore from laughing so hard at that crazy Lonzi. He and Eric together were a hot mess because Eric was just as funny, but in a different way. Eric wasn't what you would call a queen.

Lonzi had a husband named Rick. They had been together for about thirteen years and decided to go to Canada to get married. I guess it's true when they say opposites attract because those two were really different from one another.

For starters, Rick was quiet and laid back compared to Lonzi, who was flamboyant and a true diva. Then you had their careers. Lonzi was a hair stylist and Rick was very conservative and worked a corporate job. It was hard to believe they were a couple, because Rick didn't act gay, but they definitely were together.

At some point I began looking forward to seeing Lonzi, and I found myself missing him when he didn't make it to the shop. I looked forward to Fridays when he normally came through. There are some people in this world who have a gift for just lighting up your life.

Lonzi and I became friends quickly. We started going out to eat often, and even that was an adventure. People's heads would turn when Lonzi passed them, because lawd have mercy, Lonzi was such a sight to see.

Mealtime with Lonzi was something else, honey. His favorite restaurant was a place called Houston's. Everybody who was somebody in Atlanta dined at Houston's. Sometimes we would get there around 1:00 p.m. or so and not leave until after 5:00 p.m.! The whole time we'd be in there, people were constantly stopping at our table to talk to Lonzi.

It seemed as if everybody knew him, and the ones who didn't know him still had something to say. I remember this one hilarious time when I was out having lunch with him and this random woman approached our table.

"Excuse me," the woman said to Lonzi.

"Yes, baby," Lonzi replied in his high-pitched tone.

"Aren't you from that television show?"

Honey, Lonzi didn't flinch or show any sign of dishonesty when he answered this woman.

"Yes I am, dear." He didn't even know what show she was talking about.

"Wow, I'm so happy to meet you. Can I have your autograph?" The food was literally about to come out of my mouth. I held in my laugh with all my might.

"Sweetie, I would love to give you my autograph, but I'm in the middle of a meal." She apologized and walked off.

"Lonzi, what show was she talking about?" I asked him.

"I don't know, but hell, it sounded good," he replied.

Leave it up to Lonzi. He was always somebody: a music producer, model, actor, or dancer. He just went right along with it and never missed a beat. We had a ball.

Lonzi often came to pick me up from the shop when it was slow, so we could hang out, which was usually on a Monday or Tuesday. One day we were walking, and Lonzi just stopped and looked at me and said, "Miss Kim. Girl, you know I love you, and you are cute and everything, but girl, your butt is as flat as a wall. You know you got the pancake syndrome."

I started cracking up laughing, but I also knew he was telling the truth. That butt that I always longed for, like Mama Essie's, never came.

I looked up at Lonzi and said, "Sissy, be quiet."

He chuckled, but then said something that I will never forget. "It's okay, Ms. Kim, because one day you gon' really love you some Lonzi."

"I already do, but what do you mean?" I asked.

"Oh, you'll see soon. I'll tell you, friend, when it's time."

Lonzi was always so extra. I'd have gray hairs if I tried to decipher everything he said. I just shrugged the comment off as we went about our day. I knew whatever he said had some truth behind it. It was only a matter of time before I found out exactly what he meant.

Chapter 3

Secret Hustle

After my mom went through a divorce from her abusive husband, I went to live with her. I was happy to finally be reunited with my mom. From the first grade to the fourth grade, I was the only black kid in my elementary school. Boy, the white kids used to torture me about being black. I dreaded going to school each day. I was glad when the school day ended. Racism still had a very strong presence in Georgia back in the early '70s.

My mom worked for General Motors on the assembly line, and for my sixth birthday, she bought me a canopy bed. That bed was every little girls' dream bed back then. It was the one in the Sears catalog, antique white. I remember it like it was just yesterday. I told my classmates that I had gotten that bed, and my teacher overheard me talking to them. She called me to her desk and told me to, "Stop telling your untruths, because I know that you don't really have that bed." I kept telling her that I did have the bed. So I went home and told my mom, and she went right up to the school the next day and 'cussed' the teacher out. Of course, the teacher wasn't very nice to me after that. But my mom raised me to always speak my mind, and I was taught to stand up for myself.

By the sixth grade, because it was just my mom and me, she decided to teach me how to drive. Me and my little, young eleven-year-old self was behind the wheel of a real car.

By age twelve, I was driving all around the city of Atlanta. I know it may sound crazy, but my mom had a reason behind the madness. She explained that if she were to ever get sick, I should be able to drive her to the hospital. Hey, it made sense to me.

My cousins and I were driving around Atlanta in a big ole Ford Station Wagon. It was truly a sight to see. And to some, I'm sure it sounds unbelievable.

Time went on, and I eventually went to high school. Still, I found myself dealing with the same struggles against racism, but only more intensely because these offenders were teenagers. Racism and jealousy were a bad mix, and the jealousy really began to show when my mom bought me a car at the age of sixteen.

I was already fighting the prejudices from my white peers, but now the jealousy was also coming from the black kids who I thought were my friends. Kids were saying, "Yeah, Kim thinks she's all that." Even some of my own family members felt that way. The whole situation was annoying, and I started to act out and became rebellious, because to me, I was ALL THAT.

Two years earlier, at fourteen my friends and I started going out to nightclubs. Sometimes we'd go to teen clubs, which were a big deal in the early '80s. And other times we'd go to the adult clubs to drink and smoke weed and dance. My mom worked at night, so I always had a lot of freedom.

My friends always wore tight jeans and cute little dresses, showing off their nice butts. I, on the other hand, didn't feel comfortable. I'd wear something loose. And the shirt had to be long, or I had to have on a jacket to cover my shape. I got teased for having a flat butt, so I made sure to keep it covered.

Even as I got older, as a nineteen or twenty-year-old young lady, I was in the club wearing business attire. I just didn't feel like I had that "flaunt it" shape, so instead I hid it. I made up for it by always showing cleavage.

I knew Lonzi's comments about my backside weren't coming from a mean place, but they reminded me of a time when I was teased about my shape.

Men wouldn't pay me much attention and headed straight to the big booty sistas. I mostly heard comments like, "Man, she's cute, but that ass is flat." My friends heard them too, and felt bad and tried to make me feel better. They'd say things to lighten the mood. "Girl, your hair is so cute," or "You have got such a pretty face." I felt all of that was to compensate for the way I was feeling. It reminded me of my hair incident and how I was proud of my afro. Then my mother's opinion made me feel like something was wrong. Now my friends were doing the same thing. They all made me even more self-conscious, whether they meant to or not.

When everybody wore those little short shorts in the early '80s, honey, I wouldn't dare. Lonzi had reiterated something that I already felt was a flaw, when he brought up my flat butt. But it was okay. One day, maybe I could do something about it.

Not long after Lonzi's crack about me having the flat butt syndrome, I attended an event with him and Rick that led to a great discovery. In fact, it helped make my wish for a bigger backside become a stronger possibility.

Every year, Lonzi and his hubby Rick traveled to Chicago to attend the "Miss Global" pageant, held during Labor Day weekend. It was a beauty pageant for gays, similar to Miss America or Miss USA. The pageant involved mostly transsexuals or transvestites. Transsexuals are people who have actually had surgery to change their sex. Transvestites are individuals who dress the part, but don't go through the entire process. They are pre-op, meaning they have the breasts and hips only, but not the actual genitalia. In order to be in the pageant, they had to be pre-op.

I knew the pageant would be a sight to see, and I really wanted to go. Besides, I had never been to Chicago.

Along with attending the pageant every year, Lonzi and Rick also sponsored a contestant. Honey, when I tell you they went all out, that's an understatement. They put their all and then some into their contestant. "She" always won something, guaranteed. If she didn't win in any of the several categories she participated in, she almost always won the evening gown category.

Lonzi and Rick wouldn't spare a penny on their contestant. They had her gown custom made from the finest materials and exclusive tailors and seamstresses in Italy or China. If they didn't go that route, they would purchase her "fab," as Lonzi called it, from an exclusive boutique that he knew would undoubtedly win. And he was right, because his participants always did!

The two of them really cherished this event, and they talked about it with so much flare and enthusiasm, I figured I couldn't miss it. I told Lonzi that I just had to go. He was too excited to have me tag along. This would be my first time in Chi-town, so I was really looking forward to the trip.

Lonzi really impressed me with the way he handled things. Especially the way he was dropping big money. Now mind you, I knew Lonzi was doing something besides hair, but I just wasn't sure what. I figured he had some down low hustle going on, but I never knew what it was exactly. I had my hunches. Honestly, I assumed he did credit cards or checks. You know, credit card scams, where someone could charge thousands of dollars' worth of merchandise with a fake credit card or check. Several gay men were known for that kind of stuff. Chile, please! You know some of them are known for pulling all kinds of stunts when it comes to doing something illegal, but I've never been one to judge.

I was very direct with Lonzi. Since we were close, I'd ask him what he was doing on the side. "Now, Ms. Kim, why I gotta keep telling you to stay up outta my Kool Aid? When the time comes I will tell your nosy behind," he said.

"Umm umm um! Girl, when he tells you, you gon' trip out," Eric said.

Those two were something else. Of course the secrecy of the whole thing sparked an even stronger interest to find out what in the world Lonzi was doing. You know what they say about curiosity, and curiosity was about to kill this cat.

Bay-bee, Chicago was absolutely beautiful. It is a wonderful city. Awe-gazing skyscrapers, five-star restaurants, and plenty of high-end retail. Lonzi explained we'd be staying on Michigan Avenue, and honey when I tell you Lonzi knew how to ball, he knew how to ball! When we pulled up to the hotel, chile I was blown away! It was fabulous. Top of the line. Oprah even sent her guests there.

Whenever I was with Lonzi, he made sure I got the total red carpet treatment. The whole package. He paid for a masseuse to come to my room and I got the best massage. I then went to the spa and got the platinum treatment. Honey, by the time I left I felt like a new person.

My suite was across the hall from his and Rick's suite. He was keeping me entertained with the hotel's little luxuries because he said he'd be busy for about four or five hours. I decided to take a nap, and after that massage, I think I fell into the mattress.

When I woke up, I decided to go fill my ice bucket. I opened the door and I bumped into these two tall women. I remember thinking, Dang, the WNBA must be staying here because those are some big ol' women. I had to take a second look. I just had to. When I looked into one of their faces, I noticed how big her cheeks were. Super jaws. They looked like chipmunk cheeks.

You know I just had to look down. What woman do you know who wears a size 13 or 14 shoe? Well, that's what size their feet looked like. Dang, they had some big feet! I quickly kept my head down and headed toward the ice machine. When I was far enough away, I turned and glanced back. The two of them were standing outside of Lonzi's door.

"I should have known," I said out loud. "One of them must be the contestant they are sponsoring."

I completed my mission and went back to my room. Time was going quickly, but boredom had set in. I looked up at the clock and already six hours had gone by. I wasn't sure if Lonzi and Rick were asleep, or otherwise occupied, so I decided to call over to their room.

Rick answered and the conversation went something like this:

"I am so bored over here. What are y'all doing?"

"Well, baby, Lonzi's a little tied up right now and—"

Suddenly I heard Lonzi yelling in the background. "Tell her to come on over because I'm just about finished. I just need ten more minutes."

"Well, you heard him." Rick laughed. "See you in a few minutes."

We ended the call, and I waited a little more than ten minutes before going over. When I walked into their room, I was thoroughly impressed. I must've had the baby suite, because I had a nice sized sitting area in my room. But Lonzi and Rick must have had the penthouse version, because their room was huge! Everything he did was top-notch.

When I walked in, Rick told me to have a seat. He sounded more like his executive assistant rather than his husband. I didn't pay it any attention really. I was used to Lonzi's dramatized antics. Rick explained that Lonzi was still tied up, and he'd be done in a few minutes.

I heard Lonzi talking to someone in the distance, and from the sound of that pseudo-feminine voice, I knew he was speaking to a drag queen. I made some small talk with Rick about the pageant and so forth. All of a sudden, I heard something very strange coming from Lonzi's room. Whoever it was sounded like they were in distress.

"Oh Lonzi, oh Lonzi. It hurts! It hurts so bad, Lonzi. I can't do this. Ohhh, ohhh. Okay Lonzi . . . STOPPP. Please STOPPP!"

By this time I was tripping out because I didn't know what was going on. Rick was sitting there like he hadn't heard a thing. I was trying to act like I didn't hear it, but I couldn't hold back my thoughts. I looked at Rick and wondered, Oh my God! What kind of mess y'all got going on up in here? My heart pounded quick from nervousness.

Then I heard moans and someone saying, "I can't take it. Oh God, I can't take the pain, Lonzi!" The person sounded like they were crying. Okay, for real . . . by now I was tripping real hard. I was about to run up outta there full speed. And Rick had the nerve to still be talking like we were having a normal conversation with no raunchy noises coming from that back room. This was a whole new level of crazy.

"What in the world is Lonzi doing?" I finally asked Rick. I was trying to stay calm, but my palms were sweating like crazy!

Rick said, "Oh, girl, you don't know?"

"Heck no, I don't know. Know what?"

Rick got up and went into the back room where the noises of despair were coming from. He quickly returned.

"Girl, Lonzi said to come on back." My heart was racing, chile. I was walking so slowly because I didn't have a clue what the heck I was about to see. It took a long time to get back there. Actually, I was afraid.

When I finally walked in, what I saw was crazy. Lonzi had the nerve to have on a doctor's white coat, gloves, and had someone lying across the hotel desk that he'd converted into a surgical station.

The "patient" was lying on his stomach with his pants down. His bare behind was in the air. Lonzi stood behind him with a syringe in his hand. My mouth fell wide open.

"Lonzi, what in the world are you doing!"

He looked back at me without a care in the world and said, "Making magic, Ms. Kim. You didn't know I was a magician, did you, girl?"

And that's how I found out about Lonzi's secret hustle. He was doing butt-enhancement injections. I watched about ten to fifteen drag queens see Lonzi in the time we were in Chicago. They all wanted their butts done. I was shocked. In awe. Honey, I simply couldn't believe it.

Chapter 4

Fatty Over Flatty

The transgender community were first to lead the way toward the backroom butt-injection scene in the 1980s and '90s. For a male transitioning to a female at that time, it was absurd to think an insurance company would pay for the procedure. The black market became the outpatient surgical office for this type of cosmetic enhancement because it was more economical. Also, at the time, the fat-transfer method had yet to be developed. To get the desired results for a round, feminine butt, injections were the preferred method for many in the transgender community. Once some of these women made their transitions, they employed themselves as butt doctors, using the same injection procedure utilized on their own bodies.2

The revelation of Lonzi's business was one of the few things in this world that left me speechless. I just could not believe it. Lonzi did their cheeks, breasts, hips, legs and of course their butts.

After I got over the initial shock, curiosity set in big time, honey. I wasn't interested in anything but the booty. My mind had conjured up all these questions. I wanted to know how it worked. How did the butt get bigger? How much did it cost? And of course, last but not least, how could I get one?

At that time, I wasn't concerned at all about the health risks. Honey, I couldn't have cared less if there were any risks at all, and I had no clue if there were any. I just knew one thing: I wanted one, and I wanted it like yesterday. Then I started to imagine how I would look after I had the process done.

Imagining how I would look was not something new to me because I'd already envisioned myself with a flat stomach too. I'd wanted an abdominoplasty (tummy tuck) for quite a while. My two children had done a job on my stomach. Both pregnancies left me with a flabby belly full of stretch marks. Baby, I would wear not one, but two girdles to suck it all in. The problem with the girdles was that they not only held in my stomach, but my booty too. And that was definitely a NO-NO! I didn't want my butt any flatter than it already was. Lonzi's business had really given me some food for thought.

I truly had a ball with Lonzi and Rick in Chicago that weekend. The pageant was everything they described it to be. I couldn't even tell that some of the contestants were not truly women. They looked good. Really good. You better believe I bugged Lonzi all weekend about the shots. I wanted to know every detail. All he said was, "Now, Miss Kim. Girl, I told you we would twalk later." Yes honey, TWALK! That was Lonzi's way of saying we would walk and talk about it later. But I didn't want to wait. He was taunting me because he knew how anxious I was.

"Just tell me the basics," I whined, harassing my friend.

"Miss Kim, when we 'eew and chew' I will let you know, okay?" I stomped my feet and whined like a spoiled child. 'Eew and chew' was another saying from Lonzi's special vocabulary book, and that's what he called us going out to eat. He came up with the term because whenever we went out to eat, I'd be chewing my food and saying "eew" at the same time because of all the juicy drama and gossip Lonzi told me. So the new name for going out to eat was 'eew and chew.' Lonzi was too funny.

When we finally got back to Atlanta . . . humph . . . you already know. I was on a mission. I got on the ball and was determined to find a plastic surgeon to do my tummy tuck. All I kept thinking was how good I'd feel having a nice, flat stomach and cute round butt. I'd take a fatty over a flatty any day.

Lonzi told me about this plastic surgeon he knew. He said only good things about him, so I was interested in setting up a consultation. I asked Lonzi how he knew him, and he said, "Now, Miss Kim, what is the problem? You ask too many questions. Just trust me." I asked him to make me an appointment for a consultation. This was serious surgery, and I wasn't about to quit bugging Lonzi for details about this doctor. Since I would be put under anesthesia, I wanted to know everything that Lonzi knew about this doctor. I didn't want a quack operating on me, so the details were important.

Finally, Lonzi told me he knew the doctor because he used to work in his office. He explained that he and the doctor were still close. All I kept thinking was, Lonzi does butts and he isn't a doctor. So this doctor that I'm going to see about my stomach better be the real deal!

Actually, I found that this doctor's office was where Lonzi learned how to do his 'magic,' as he liked to call it. He accompanied me to the consultation. I was so excited and nervous at the same time. Thankfully, the surgeon made me feel very comfortable about the process. He and Lonzi talked and laughed the entire time, which made me feel better.

There are several cosmetic procedures being done these days. He was a very good doctor and was board certified. He had the skills to do different types of cosmetic surgical procedures.

I picked up a book with some before and after pictures of his work and was impressed. He did many rhinoplasties. A rhinoplasty is a nose job. I could see the great work he'd done once I looked at the before and after pictures of some his patients. He made a big difference with their overall facial appearance.

One woman had a huge bump on her nose. Not a bump like a pimple, but a bump caused by her bone structure. The new nose was a major improvement. It was smooth, and you couldn't tell she had any work done to it.

Another picture was of a woman's labia, also known as vaginal lips. The before pictures showed them to be uneven and quite large. I flinched when I saw that one. It took me a moment to realize what I was looking at. The description written beneath the photo explained what she had done. She had a labioplasty and vaginoplasty. The labioplasty part of the procedure is where the labia (lips) are cut and shaped to look pretty and not like two wrinkled elephant ears. The vaginoplasty actually tightened the vagina itself. Sometimes childbirth and frequent sex can loosen the muscles of the vaginal walls. This procedure reversed that, and tightened everything back up. Technology was something.

I turned the page to continue browsing, and I saw the droopiest little breasts I had ever seen. It didn't look like there was any help for this woman, but this doctor was a transformer. The after photos were really on point. Honey, this woman now had a million dollar rack. The notes beneath this picture showed that she'd had breast augmentation, and the saline bags were placed beneath the muscle, giving them a very convincing look and authentic feel.

There were many more pictures, but another one that struck me was of a woman who had the same procedure I was looking to have done. Her stomach was hanging over her panties and she had thick stretch marks all over her belly. Every woman's afterbirth nightmare has that same look. It was not a pretty sight. Then, there were the after the surgery photos right next to it. If it were not for the tattoo on her stomach, I would not have known it was the same person. It looked like her waist size went from a thirty-six to a twenty-six.

Immediately, I got excited all over again and wanted to show Lonzi. But he was busy making small talk with the receptionist, so I just kept on flipping pages. The work was very impressive. Honey, I turned the page again and got the biggest shock of my life. Lo and behold, there was a page with Lonzi's before and after photos. It showed Lonzi's face prior to the surgery. I tried . . . I swear I tried to hold in my laughter, but I could not. I cracked up. I laughed so hard tears came to my eyes. I just couldn't stop, and I had actually gotten a little loud. Other patients turned to look at me, but please, I did not care. This was a moment to be remembered. I was unable to breathe. Those pictures were beyond hysterical. He even had the nerve to have a Jheri curl.

Lonzi walked over to me to see what all the commotion was about. He said, "Miss Kim, what is wrong with you, girl?" I lifted the book up and showed him. If there had been glass in the room, it would have definitely cracked. Lonzi let out a shriek so loud, Mariah Carey couldn't have hit a higher note. He dramatically snatched the book out of my hands and put the whole binder inside his purse. Yes, he took the poor doctor's book showcasing all of his work.

As he was stuffing it in his oversized bag, I asked, "Lonzi, are you crazy?"

"Nobody can ever, ever see those pictures, Miss Kim," he threatened. I just could not stop laughing. I cracked up all over again, but Lonzi did not have even the slightest smirk on his face. He was dead serious, and it was too funny.

Finally, I completed my consultation. I was a healthy candidate for the tummy tuck. Before any doctor does an abdominoplasty, they examine you thoroughly. I told the doctor I would schedule the surgery as soon as I arranged for someone to watch my children.

When we left the doctor's office, honey, Lonzi was still tripping out about those before and after photos. You know I had to tease him. I told him it was all-good and he just used to be an ugly duckling and now he was a beautiful, black swan. Of course, he didn't see the humor in anything I said, but I thought it was pretty funny.

He looked me dead in my eyes without cracking a smile or blinking and swore me to secrecy. I agreed and continued to laugh. I told him not to feel bad because I was getting ready to have surgery too, and if he had not taken the book, we would have been in there together. Well, that's as long as the cosmetic surgeon didn't screw up my surgery.

Chapter 5

Perfectly Plump

Lonzi was Mr. Popular when it came to butt enhancements. Now that I knew what it was that he was doing, he would take me with him to work. On several occasions I watched him fatten up peoples' behinds. Mostly drag queens though. Some of them had supermodel bodies.

The more I watched, the more I wanted to get it done myself. I was only a couple weeks away from getting my tummy tuck. So Lonzi insisted I work on my butt before the surgery. I agreed to let him "fix" me up, but in the back of my mind, I was thinking, Chile, I ain't even sure there is any help for this butt.

I went out and grabbed a couple of black magazines known for showcasing voluptuous backsides, like Smooth and King, and they had no shortage of butts. With those images in mind, I tried to get a mental picture of what I thought my butt should look like. I wanted it to be round and soft. Not too wide, not too narrow, just perfectly plump.

Literally, I drove myself crazy doing all that imagining. Finally, I thought, Kim, girl, calm down. Any booty is better than the one you got. So just be grateful. The butt I had was . . . well, no butt at all.

I was scared. Yeah, I must admit I was very nervous. Chile, the night before, I tossed and turned something terrible. I didn't get any sleep. The anxiety I felt was intense. In the morning, I'd be a new woman. Miss New Booty. I would have the one look I always wanted.

Bright and early I arrived at Lonzi's place that could have been featured in any magazine. It was absolutely gorgeous. His home was immaculate at all times and furnished to the tee. It looked like something Liberace would dwell in. It was definitely Lonzi's style, gaudy and over the top. When they vacuumed, the carpet had to have the perfect pattern. The lines were straight like a manicured lawn. So straight, I didn't even want to walk across it. Even the furniture seemed only for show. It seemed too elegant to be seated on. But if you knew Lonzi, you knew not to expect anything less than the best. He was such a trip that at Christmastime he would have someone decorate his entire house. A Christmas tree adorned every room that had a window facing the street. That was Lonzi.

Upstairs, Lonzi had an office set up in his house. I remember the first time I walked up the staircase to get to that room. We can call it Lonzi's 'operating room.' Many people probably felt brand new leaving out of this very same space. My nerves were going, but I was here and there was no turning back.

The room was prepped for the procedure. He had completely transformed his office. I had never seen it as it looked now. Lonzi had everything ready. He prepared a table I assumed was for me. Next to the table was a smaller table where he placed the supplies. There were a few items that I'd seen Lonzi use many times before. I just had a different reaction knowing that those very same items were now going to be used on me.

"We're all for you," is what I heard those cotton balls, the syringe, and needle all shout out to me. There was also medical glue, gel, gloves, and gauze pads on the table as well. Man was I scared.

Lonzi instructed me to take my pants off and climb onto the makeshift operating table. I had on a thong, so I kept it on. My nerves were really working overtime now. I felt like I might pee on myself at any moment and had to literally squeeze my kegel muscles to keep from going right there. Sweat beaded up on my face and everything.

"Lawd, what have I gotten myself into?" I whispered. I'd seen the procedure done several times, but honey, nothing prepares you for having it done yourself. So many things run through your mind. But I can surely tell you one thing, no thought is more prevalent than the one that reminds you of what you're about to look like once it's all done. A bootylicious diva, and that was all that really mattered.

I tried to relax. Lonzi told me I was squeezing my butt cheeks together. I turned to look back at him, and it was like everything else in the room disappeared. All I saw was that huge needle. It seemed as if it was the longest thing I had ever seen. Lonzi told me the more I relaxed, the less I would feel it.

From my limited view, I watched Lonzi fill the syringe with a clear liquid. I never bothered to ask what it was. I was being pulled between two very strong emotions. Fear and excitement. The fear had me ready to jump off that table and run like hell. The excitement, on the other hand, had me ecstatic about getting what I'd been wanting all my life. So you know what I did? Exactly, I stayed.

In went the first stick. Honey, I can remember it like it was yesterday. Talk about painful. You have no idea. Tears slide down my face immediately. Lonzi patted my back and said, "Girlfriend, it's painful to be beautiful, and I know you ain't sitting there crying like no baby. You spit out two drive-by shooters, so you can handle this." He called kids 'drive-by shooters.' Just another one of the many sayings from Lonzi's self-made vocabulary.

I wasn't trying to hear anything about no damn labor. Every prick felt like I was being tortured. At least in labor you could get an epidural. There was no numbing in this situation. I felt every excruciating sensation, straight up, no chaser. The first cheek hurt like hell. It's not one or two sticks either. He repeated the process continually. After a while, my cheek began to numb and that helped tremendously. By the time we were half through, I was able to cope a bit better. I promised myself I was never, ever going to do this again. When he started on the other cheek, OMG the pain was back with a vengeance. Chile, labor was a cakewalk compared to this. I don't have a high tolerance for pain at all. But I wanted this and I wanted it so bad, I was willing to endure the pain. In my mind, the end justified the means.

Lonzi was steady talking to me as though he was simply putting a relaxer in one of his client's heads at the salon. My pains and moans of agony didn't seem to faze him. I came very close to quitting and still have no idea how I made it through the entire process, but I did.

Yes, I did it! I got what I wanted, and I was ready to embrace my new look. Excited, but still not completely satisfied, I felt like something was missing. I didn't know then that I had simply placed a Band-Aid over a stab wound. My insecurities were not something one simple procedure could fix. Later, I would learn that my issues were deeper than not having a plump booty. I kept my focus where it needed to be and convinced myself that I was truly happy because of what I had done. I thought I had fixed the problem. But actually, I never addressed the real root of my problems, and I wouldn't for years.

After the final injection, he placed the last cotton ball over the needle hole. It stuck to my skin because he dabbed it in some type of adhesive before sticking it on me. It kept the fluid from leaking.

When we finished, Lonzi said, "Okay, cry baby. Get up and look in the mirror." When I stood up, the first thing I noticed was that my butt felt heavier. I walked over to look at it.

"All of that pain for this?" I said, sounding disappointed. "It just looks swollen to me." After all that, I thought my butt was going to be huge.

"Calm down, Miss Kim. You'll see it soon. I contoured it to the shape of your natural ass. You know I know what I'm doing," he said. "Oh, you can't sit on your butt for at least ten hours, and don't remove the cotton balls for the same amount of time."

Baaay-bee, you should have seen me trying to drive without sitting. Let's just say that was a dangerous trip. Most of the time, when someone got injections, they brought a designated driver. I was so anxious to have the procedure done that I completely forgot about that part. Of course, I cursed Lonzi out for not reminding me.

All I wanted to do was go home and get in my bed. I was sore all over, and it felt like a dang-on truck had slammed into my ass! All that pain for this little enhancement. I was not happy.

I didn't take the cotton balls off until the next morning. I looked like Peter Cottontail. All I kept thinking was, Please let my butt look good. Well, honey, about three days later I looked in the mirror and I was definitely shocked. My butt was bootylicious for real! I now felt like it was worth every second. I know I promised myself I wouldn't go back, but that ended up being a lie. Eventually, I went back one more time.

I'd been hiding out around the house trying to stay clear of my son's father for a few days. I didn't feel like hearing his mouth. You know how men can act crazy if they think you've done something to better yourself, or if you've made an alteration that he thinks might make you more appealing to other men, especially if they're the jealous type. And believe me when I tell you my son's father was definitely the jealous type. If you look up the word jealous in the dictionary, honey, his picture would be right there taking up the entire page. Some men will say to their women, "Why did you lose so much weight?" or "Why you putting on extra make-up?" Yet, they were the same ones looking at other women who did those same things. Nobody has time for that mess. He thought my butt was getting bigger because of exercise and squats. That was the lie I told because I felt it wasn't his business to know.

Anyway, my butt was perfect, and I couldn't remember ever feeling so good about myself in my life. It seemed it had grown tremendously in those three days. Lonzi told me it would happen, and I honestly didn't believe him. Now the proof was in the pudding, baby. There was a new Kimberly Smedley, and nobody could tell me anything.

I went back to work and didn't want anybody to know what I had done. I started wearing baggy clothes to hide my body. Chile, please! That didn't work though, because as soon as I walked into the shop, everybody knew. Lonzi told the whole salon. He couldn't help himself. You know what they say, Telegram, Telephone, Tell-a-Sissy! I wasn't upset; I just didn't want my son's father to know. Fortunately, I was able to keep it from him. Still, it wasn't Lonzi's place to tell my personal business. How did I know he wouldn't do that with something even more secretive?

Chapter 6
The Self-Esteem Aspect

Jeans, jogging suits, pencil skirts, summer dresses, honey, you name it, I rocked it and rocked it well. My confidence skyrocketed, and I woke up every day feeling so good about myself. Going to the mall was an entirely new experience. I loved trying on clothes and showing off my new figure. It was hard not to catch me with a smile on my face. Some men that weren't looking my way before were now taking double and triple takes. It really felt good.

Self-esteem and self-love are truly important. When you look in the mirror and truly love what you see, it changes everything. In a perfect world, we would easily ignore our so-called flaws, but we do not live in a perfect world. We live in a judgmental, cruel, and fad-based society. With technology and scientific advances at an all-time high, we can make a lot of alterations to ourselves. But there is such a thing as going too far.

Truly I was happy with my results, but I can admit I made some mistakes. Safety and long-term possible health risks were not a concern of mine when I was getting the procedure done. I was unhappy with a part of my body and I changed it, yes. But was it worth the risk of possible permanent injury or even death? When I got my tummy-tuck, a board certified surgeon did it, but my gay friend did my butt shots.

Lonzi claimed to have worked for the surgeon that did my tummy tuck and his office was where he learned to do injections. I didn't know for sure that, that was true. Even to this very day. Yes, he and the surgeon were very comfortable with each other, but I didn't fully investigate his claim. When I finally did ask Lonzi where he got the solution for the injections and what it was n of, he told me he bought it from that same doctor and it was medical grade silicone. Whenever he carried the solution, it was never in a pre-packaged container that listed all the ingredients and its FDA approved uses. All I had was Lonzi's word that it was from a surgeon, but no proof. The most interesting thing was, none of us who had the procedure done by Lonzi really cared. We trusted him.

I vowed the day I had the procedure done to never ever do it again, but that was a fallacy because I found myself back in the care of Dr. Lonzi for a few more shots to get the exact look I wanted. This was a process, folks, and once you started, you always found reasons to go back and get a little bit more. You know, let me fix this or fix that. But do we need to? And what is the powerful force that drives us to go and make these changes in the first place?

Many things females do are solely to attract the opposite sex. From our hair to the make-up we apply, to the clothes and shoes we wear, it's all about those animal instincts to attract the opposite sex. The same goes for men. Although many times we'll be quick to say, "Honey, please, I'm doing this for me and nobody else." We don't realize that, that is not the case. Many of us make these changes to alter other people's perceptions of and reactions to whom we are.

It's a sub-culture, and there is a deep history connected to having a large butt. The women of the Hottentot tribe of South Africa are known for having extremely large backsides.3 While Europeans had been starving to colonize and carve out Africa, they happened to come across this tribe. They were baffled and intrigued by these Hottentot women and their large rear ends. They actually diagnosed their large butts as a condition called steatopygia. Can you believe that? They actually saw our natural shapes as a disease.

They may have called it that then, but I can't tell today, because I've seen many white women lying across the table getting their butts enhanced too. Black women have endured many struggles and have been on the receiving end of many judgments and criticisms. Everything from the kinks in our hair, the sass in our walk, to the width of our hips. With all the controversy surrounding the butt-injections phenomenon, I can't help but think it's almost flattering to see the black women's physique being embraced.

There was a time when large bottomed female slaves were chained and forced to participate in freak shows or circuses. They were laughed at and ridiculed for their bodies. Now, those very same shapes are coveted like chocolate! With all of that being said, we can't, however, remove the self-esteem aspect from all of this. We don't see men running around getting penis implants or muscle implants at the same rate that we see women making changes to their bodies. Although male cosmetic surgery has increased tremendously over the last ten years, it still does not compare in any way to the rate of females. Why is that?

I would argue that the role women (especially black women) play in today's society can be seen as that of a sex symbol. Primarily, this is because of the cultural differences between the major two races in America. The media surely doesn't help either. Not with them constantly impressing upon us what is supposedly acceptable. Bulimia and anorexia are eating disorders that plague mostly women. A flat stomach, perky breasts, and a well-rounded derriere are what the media portrays as the ideal woman. The media's portrayal of what a woman should look like is not just a problem in America, it is a phenomenon seen all over the globe, and the specifications of what is acceptable are based on where you're from. For example, black media tends to promote a huge behind, thick thighs, a small waist, and a flat stomach is ideal. White media promotes an overall skinny figure and big breasts to be the ideal look.

I believe in being healthy, but I still see the ridiculousness in all of that. Chile, please! For all women who have had children and have breast fed, we know that imagery is often unrealistic. Whose breasts stay perky after months of nursing your baby? Whose stomach stays tight easily after nine months of your skin stretching like you swallowed a beach ball? Yes, some of us snap right back. Some of us have good genes, but not always is that the case. The pressure to keep a certain look can drive some of us ladies to do some pretty crazy things. I know this because I've heard and witnessed a few desperate situations firsthand while hanging out with Lonzi.

Chapter 7
Butt of the Joke

Like most salon's, Lonzi's place was filled with gossip, incessant chatter, sometimes a little drama and plenty of jokes. But what I didn't appreciate was being made the butt of the joke.

I started to work with Lonzi at his salon in 1997 because the salon was located closer to my home. Business was great. Lonzi and I traveled together and hung out often. I enjoyed being with him every day, well, most days.

The shop was always busy. Once, one of Lonzi's clients had come to the shop and given him a beautiful full-length mink after paying him for injections. Lonzi commented about how he would always be paid because he was the fixer. "Right, Kim?" he said and smiled.

Okay, here's the thing about cosmetic surgery: you are happy that you got it, but you don't need anybody constantly reminding you. It's annoying and insulting. The focus is no longer on your beauty enhancements; it is on the fact that you *received* beauty enhancements. Big difference.

Lonzi didn't seem to understand that. He thought anytime was an opportune moment to make me and my personal business the butt of one of his jokes. Many times I let it slide, but some days he really annoyed me. I found it to be distasteful, especially when I was already having a bad day. He really worked my nerves during those times.

You see, had I gone to a "real" surgeon, I wouldn't have had to worry about this type of crap. I would've been protected by medical privacy act laws and all that good stuff. But I was not protected under any "queen" laws because there was only one, and it was the "TELL IT ALL" law.

This particular day I had finally had enough from Lonzi, and we really had it out.

"One more comment, Lonzi, and it's gonna be my foot up your behind," I told him.

"No, it's gonna be my foot up your ass if I decide not to take it back. Ain't no warranty on that thang," he said. Everybody laughed.

"Keep on, Lonzi, and you're going to be the one crying up in here. Keep it up!" I warned.

"No, you keep it up. Don't let it deflate. I might be Dr. Fix-a-Flat, but honey, I ain't Jesus. Okay!" Lonzi just kept on being a jerk, so I fought fire with fire. I knew Lonzi thought that because he was the boss, he could say anything and get away with it. But not today. I was going to give him a taste of his own medicine.

"Okay, Lonzi, you got it. But be careful because none of us know how to put you back together once I knock you down."

"What you mean 'put me back together?' I'm together in all types of weather, sweetie!" he said, firing back.

"Yeah, Mr. Potato Head, you're together now from sewing together all those fake detachable body parts. Don't nothing on your face really belong to you. Will the real Lonzi please come out!"

The shop laughed uncontrollably.

Lonzi was livid. Honey, you could smell the smoke coming out his ears. He could dish it out, but couldn't take it. Lonzi walked away from his client, staring me down. And all I could do was laugh. I kept egging it on while styling my client's hair.

Suddenly, I felt a sharp sting and I swear I saw stars. When the stars cleared, it registered. That sissy had slapped fire out of me.

Listen, it's one thing for a female to slap you, but as feminine as Lonzi was, he was still a man and that slap hurt like hell. The whole salon got quiet.

I put my curling irons on the stove, but I didn't say anything. I just waited until they got good and hot. I walked over to Lonzi's station with the curling irons in my hand. Another stylist had been watching because she knew I wouldn't let it go. She rushed over to me and grabbed my arm and burned herself trying to keep me off Lonzi. He was lucky, because that sissy was about to be toast that day!

I packed all my things and left. That was in 1998, and I stopped talking to Lonzi for two years.

Those were two long years. I felt like I'd lost my best friend. I did lose my best friend. Yes, I'll admit that I really missed Lonzi, but I was still too angry and hurt to call him. He was flat out wrong and I felt he needed to apologize. On several occasions, Eric, my friend from the old salon where I worked would call me and say, "Kim, you really need to call Lonzi because he's been sick."

I told Eric, "If he isn't dead, he can pick up the phone and call me." I dismissed Lonzi being sick as him being a drama queen as usual. "Whatever!"

In 2000, out of the blue, Lonzi called me. I was shocked. He told me he was very sorry, and if he could take it back, he would. Instantly, I accepted his apology without any hesitation. I was tired of being stubborn and prideful, so I was happy he took the initiative to reinstate our friendship. He asked me to go on a trip with him to Detroit and I agreed. I thought it would be good for us. I could always use a little "eew and chew!" He told me we could make it a bonding trip, even though it was going to be work. He was still doing butt injections.

Lonzi took care of the flight arrangements, and then he called to give me our itinerary. I was excited to be linking back up with him.

The day we were leaving for Detroit, I agreed to meet Lonzi at his house. I hadn't been there in a long time, and it instantly brought back some fond memories.

When I arrived, Rick opened the door and embraced me. He called out to Lonzi to let him know I was there. All I could think of was which Versace outfit Lonzi would be wearing, and which purse he would be carrying today. I knew it would be extra since we were traveling and had to go through the airport. I was eager to see my old friend.

For a moment I thought my eyes were playing tricks on me. As Lonzi was walking down those stairs, I almost said out loud, "What the h—who is that?" I couldn't believe it. The Lonzi I knew was so full of life, flamboyant, funny, and a top-notch diva. The man I saw couldn't have weighed more than 100 pounds, and that was soaking wet. My God!

This couldn't be Lonzi! The man coming down the stairs looked nothing like the Lonzi I knew. I glanced at Rick and he just put his head down. Lonzi's face was sunken in and he was very weak. It seemed to hurt him to simply walk down the stairs. This wasn't Lonzi. I was completely caught off guard and in total shock.

I'd heard a few things during the time we weren't speaking, but nothing like this. I'd heard Lonzi had been hospitalized a few times with pneumonia and other illnesses, but I had no idea it was this bad. A deep sadness had come over me. I tried not to let it show because I didn't want to upset him, or make him feel uncomfortable.

During the ride to the airport, we filled each other in on what had been going on in our lives. There was so much to talk about. He asked about my boys; he was always very fond of them.

"Miss Kim, how are those drive-by shooters of yours? Especially that youngest one that looks just like you? Is he still bad as hell?"

I laughed, because Lonzi always had a witty, crazy way of speaking. I knew he didn't mean any harm. You just had to understand Lonzi's sense of humor. He always told me how he admired the relationship I had with my kids. He knew they were truly my everything.

Once we arrived at the airport and had to walk all the way to the terminal, I realized how weak Lonzi was. We stopped many times so he could regain himself. I wasn't sure if we would make it to our gate. A five minute walk took Lonzi over twenty minutes.

Finally, we boarded the plane, but Lonzi was out of breath and sweating like he had just finished running a twenty mile marathon. I wanted to talk to him some more because I needed to know what was wrong. I was hoping Lonzi had a bad case of the flu or something and disprove what I had heard and what my mind was telling me.

We ended up not doing much talking at all because Lonzi slept majority of the flight. None of this was what I expected. I just knew I'd be cracking up laughing, clowning and conversing with my friend like we used to do. Instead, I found myself praying and checking to make sure he was okay.

When I agreed to take this trip with Lonzi, I had no idea this would be the trip that changed my life forever. I learned some things that set many courses for my future.

That afternoon we arrived at the hotel and checked in. As usual, Lonzi had us at the best of the best. The people at the front desk knew who he was and quickly checked us in. When we exited the elevator, honey, let me tell you. There was a line of clients waiting along both walls outside his suite.

They all looked excited and nervous, the same way people always did right before they got their injections. Some said they had been waiting since 5:00 a.m. There were a lot of people waiting, and I knew it was going to be a very long day.

When we finally got into the room, Lonzi looked really bad. His skin appeared ashen. He told me he felt very weak and needed to eat right away. I quickly ordered room service. He would definitely need his strength if he was going to work on all those people waiting outside the room.

Poor Lonzi couldn't even finish his food. He took a few bites, but then felt nauseated. I laid him down and rushed to the bathroom to wet a washcloth with cool water. After I placed it on his forehead, I stroked his head, hoping it would make him feel better. He said he only needed a few minutes to get himself together. I didn't have a clue as to what I was supposed to do. I was so nervous and I started praying, "Lord, please help Lonzi."

I didn't know what I was going to tell these people. Clients had come from all over, near and far. Later, I learned that some had come from Ohio and Chicago, and they would have been quite pissed if they had come to Detroit for nothing.

I went into the hallway, and the questions were thrown at me like footballs.

"How much longer?"

"Do I need to pee first?"

"Is Lonzi all right?"

"How long is this gonna take?"

"Who are you?"

"You know I was first."

Honey, I didn't know what to do. The questions just kept coming. I said the first thing that came to mind. I told them Lonzi was on an important business call, and he would be right with them.

I went back in the room and Lonzi had fallen asleep. *What now?* I thought. I didn't want to wake him, so I let him sleep for about twenty minutes since I was able to calm the clients down. Eventually, they started knocking on the door.

"Lonzi," I whispered. "Lonzi, baby, you've got people waiting, and they are starting to get restless. I'm going to let the first client in, okay?" He gave me a weak-approving nod. I let the lady in.

This suite had a big conference table. Rather than have the client lie on the bed, I told her to lie on the table. Lonzi got himself together while I set up the supplies. He was moving so slow.

He filled the syringe with clear fluid and began the injections. His hand trembled so badly, I assisted him by placing the glue over the injection site and sticking the cotton ball on it. He would stick and I would seal. We had a little routine going.

Lonzi began to inject again, and as he was putting the fluid in this woman's butt, he leaned to the side and vomit in the trashcan. It smelled horrible, but Lonzi couldn't stop. He continued to do the injections, but kept throwing up the entire time.

"Oh my God!" I murmured.

Usually, the procedure would take twenty to thirty minutes because he worked quickly, but it took Lonzi an entire hour to finish the first client. Lawd have mercy, honey. Lonzi was throwing up and injecting the lady at the same time. And she didn't even make him stop! She allowed a sick man to work on her with a needle and a syringe. I felt so bad. Now that I think about it, it's not like she had much of a choice, unless she was going to leave there with one cheek bigger than the other.

I knew when Lonzi was napping that I should've just let him sleep and cancelled the clients. I did try, but he wouldn't let me. You know something ain't right when he had to lie down after *every* client. That's how bad he was.

I tried my best to help him finish up. He made it through about six more clients before exhaustion set in. He collapsed onto the bed, looked up at me, and said, "Miss Kim, you've gotta finish my clients."

"I can't do that," I told him.

"But you have to, Miss Kim," he said.

I didn't know what to say. But I knew one thing, that moment was the end of one phase of my life and the beginning of another.

Chapter 8

Tomorrow is not Promised

Lonzi was so weak he could hardly move. That was scary. "Please, Miss Kim, please. I can't leave all of those clients hanging. Girl, I need your help."

I kindly declined. "Lonzi, you know I love you, but I can't. I have no idea what I'm supposed to be doing," I explained.

Up until this point, all I'd ever done was watch Lonzi. I mean, I would place a cotton ball over a hole or fill up the syringe, but I had never actually done an injection. I was afraid of needles.

As Lonzi continued to insist, and the clients' impatience grew, I gave in and told him I would try.

After I scrubbed my hands and arms, I got a pair of latex gloves and put them on like I often saw Lonzi do. I siked myself up to do the injections, only because I knew if I didn't, it could reflect badly on Lonzi. I went out into the hallway and let the next client in.

This woman came in and I explained that Lonzi wasn't feeling well and if she wanted to reschedule she could, or if she wanted to get the procedure done, I would have to do it.

Honey, she didn't care at all. She dropped her pants and lay across that table. Lonzi gave me step by step instructions as I began administering the shots. It was very obvious I had never done this by the way Lonzi was talking to me. You would think the client would be concerned or worried that an inexperienced stranger was injecting her, but she never said a word. She just lay there. I didn't comprehend the mindset she must have had that allowed her to go through with it.

She never inquired about my medical background, or if I ever had any medical training. This was a level of desperation that even I wouldn't have sunk to in my time of despair. The clients just wanted what they wanted and that was that.

After the first one, I was still tripping about administering the injections. All kinds of crazy thoughts raced through my head, and I started voicing them to Lonzi. He just told me it was going to be okay, and I was doing fine. I am not sure if he really meant it. It may have been his illness talking.

As the clients continued to come in and get their injections, Lonzi managed to stay alert to instruct me well enough so I could get through each person. He explained the needle must be inserted a certain way to avoid the migration of the silicone.

Migration is when silicone fluid moves from the original injection site to another location. I had to be very careful because the biggest risk was the silicone getting into the bloodstream by hitting a vein or main artery. He explained the risk of hitting a vein was very low since the butt was mostly fat. Lonzi also told me the only blood I should see should be a small amount from the needle piercing the skin. Nothing drastic. A large amount of blood meant a vein or artery was struck, and I should pull out because the fluid could go into the person's lungs. I tried to be a good student and listened to everything he said. It was a lot to take in at once.

So far, so good. That day I was able to finish all Lonzi's clients. It was a slow, tedious process, but each one endured the pain. Some of them even encouraged me. They all looked so happy afterward. I could relate to the feeling myself. But all I thought was, *Is it that serious that these women let me do their butts, and they knew it was my first time?* I didn't understand why .

Unfortunately, as the night went on, Lonzi had gotten much worse. I tried everything, but Lonzi was out of it. He kept throwing up. Nothing I did helped. I didn't know what else to do. Lonzi refused to go to the emergency room.

By then I decided to call Rick because I figured he'd know what to do, or could at least talk Lonzi into going to the hospital. I was very scared. Rick was upset. He told me that he never wanted Lonzi to take the trip in the first place, but Lonzi insisted. When Lonzi wanted to do something, you'd have to just let him because he'd go into a tantrum.

Rick told me to get Lonzi some Pedialyte and try my best to keep him comfortable. I couldn't believe that was it. There was nothing else I could do for my friend but keep him comfortable? I sat next to him in disbelief and held back my tears, feeling so helpless.

When I returned from the store, he was still asleep. I could tell he had still been throwing up. I ordered him some chicken soup and gave him the Pedialyte to drink. He was in bad shape.

I called Eric. "I believe Lonzi is dying," I told him directly, before I broke down and cried.

"What the heck do you mean?" Eric asked.

I explained that I was in Detroit with Lonzi and what was going on.

Eric said, "What! Ms. Thang, you better get Lonzi back here now! What the hell are you doing out of town with him? I told you he was sick, fool!"

I packed all our things so I could get us back to the 'A.' The entire time I was packing, I kept checking on Lonzi and praying silently, nonstop. *God, please don't let Lonzi die on me. Please!*

The next morning we left in a hurry. Lonzi was still vomiting. To be exact, he'd never stopped since the day before. Just imagine watching someone throw up for about ten hours straight. Really just heaving because there was nothing left on his stomach.

At the airport, I got Lonzi a wheelchair. There was no way he could walk any place at all. Once we boarded the plane, I felt relieved that we were on our way back.

He lay across the seat and spread out. It was a pretty empty flight, so we had an extra seat between the two of us. Poor Lonzi was curled up in the fetal position. All I did was cry. I couldn't stop, because I had my regrets.

I wished I hadn't wasted two years being mad with Lonzi. Some things are just not worth it: holding on to a grudge or not forgiving others. Tomorrow is not promised, and Lonzi's illness really highlighted that fact.

Rather than us being angry, I wished that we'd spent more time together having fun. I should have been more rational about the situation. We wasted time, and time is something we can never get back. I held his hand the entire flight.

We finally landed, and I got him a wheelchair again at the airport. When we arrived back at Lonzi's, Rick was waiting. I helped Rick get him into bed. I wanted to stay by his side, but I had to go out of town again. It was July 2, and I promised Lonzi I'd be back by the 5th, because the guy I was dating was taking me away for the Fourth. I couldn't get Lonzi off my mind. I kept telling myself he'd be better by the time I got back. I really loved Lonzi.

While I was away, I called Rick to check on my friend. I wasn't getting an answer. Nevertheless, I kept trying because I was worried sick. Still, for the whole day I didn't get an answer. I left several messages.

The next day I called again, and I was so happy to hear Lonzi's voice. He sounded like he'd been sleeping when he answered. I hated to disturb him, but I talked to him for a little bit.

"Hey, I was just checking on you," I said.

"Miss Kim," he said, before taking a short breath, "I'm feeling a lot better, especially now that I'm hearing your voice."

"Are you resting?"

"Yes, girl"

"Did you eat?"

"Yes, honey, anything else?"

"Good. Where's Rick?"

"Honey, he went to get a haircut. Girl, you acting like you about to send somebody to rob me or something. Ohhhh, you asking a lot of questions."

I laughed. That was my Lonzi. "Be quiet and get some rest. I'll be back in a couple of days to take care of you. You know we need to catch up a little more. I love you, Lonzi."

"You know I can't wait for some 'ewwww and chew.' I love you too, Miss Kim." We both laughed, and I ended the call feeling a lot more at ease.

The next day I got a call from Rick. I don't know why, but my stomach immediately flipped and turned.

"Hello? Rick?"

"Hi Kim," Rick said in a sad tone. "Lonzi got worse throughout the night, and I rushed him to the hospital. He died from a heart attack."

I froze. Devastated. Losing Lonzi was very painful. I cried. I just couldn't believe it. He was only forty-three. Too young for something so terrible to take him away from us.

Two days later, I was given the time and location of Lonzi's funeral. I've never liked funerals. I don't know many people that do, but they are extremely difficult for me because of my father. I always felt like it tainted the memory you had of how the person looked before dying. Funerals are sad and depressing. When I was a kid, I had to go. I didn't have options then. But I did now, and I vowed that when I became an adult, I would never go to another one. However, I had to make an exception for Lonzi. There was no way I could *not* go.

His funeral was going to be held in his hometown in South Carolina, which was about three hours from Atlanta. A group of us who knew Lonzi from the salon traveled together to attend.

When we got there, baay-bee, was it packed! Everybody had turned out for Lonzi's home going. I couldn't believe how many people were there. Lonzi always used to say that when he passed, he wanted everyone to wear a big hat. He loved the elegant Kentucky Derby style hats. So I wasn't surprised when every woman and transsexual wore a hat. I smiled when I saw them. All kinds of folks showed up. People came out in droves. Straights, gays, transvestites, and transsexuals. You name the gender and they were there. Everybody wanted to pay their respects and say goodbye to the Queen, the magician, the doctor. It was standing room only, so I knew Lonzi was smiling and watching. It was beautiful, and Lonzi truly deserved such a spectacular home going. So many people were touched by Lonzi, literally. After all, he physically shaped and transformed many lives.

Honey, I couldn't stop crying, I had to admit that all the stuff Lonzi went through battling his illness while we weren't talking, scarred me. For about two weeks, I was a mess. All I could do was think and cry and cry some more. It took me a long time to get over it. Eric was there for me through it all.

From personal experience, I want to tell anyone who may be upset with, or not speaking to, or holding resentment in their heart for a loved one, to please try and let it go. I wish that I'd never wasted precious time (years that we could have created memories), being angry with him. What were the benefits? There weren't any.

But I did have our memories, our laughs, our cries, our precious moments. One thing I wished we'd done was travel to Europe. He said he always wanted to show me Europe. Lonzi would have loved that, honey. Oh yes, especially Italy or France, where all of his favorite designers came from. He went every year and told me how fabulous it was.

Life is so precious, and when someone close to you dies, it confirms and reiterates that. I'm sure if Lonzi were here today, he'd be my number one supporter.

Chapter 9

It Gets Greater Later

"Hey Kim. It's important that we talk. I need to see you as soon as possible," Rick said on one of many voice mails.

A few months had gone by, and I hadn't even heard from Rick, who was now leaving me several messages. His calls baffled my brain. *What does he want?* Lord knows I couldn't take any more bad news, but I met up with Rick because he said it was important.

"Hey Kim," he said, embracing me.

We both had to restrain our tears. "You doing all right?" he asked.

"Yes, and you?"

"I'm okay. Just trying to stay busy, so I don't think about Lonzi so much, but I need to ask you something.

"Okay, what is it?"

"Do you remember the business Lonzi was doing?"

"Of course I do. Why?"

"Well, several people have called trying to take over his business. These are people he didn't even fool with. I told all of them 'HELL NO!' Kim, you were the only person I know who Lonzi actually took out on the road with him and saw exactly what he was doing. He didn't trust everybody. Lonzi was really fond of you and loved you like a sister. He always talked about how well you were raising those boys. Girl, he thought the world of you." Rick paused. "So I figured it would only be right to leave Lonzi's business to you, if you are interested."

I immediately broke down crying. I was moved beyond words. Nobody had ever given me anything without expecting something in return. Rick's compassion touched me. For him to have acknowledged Lonzi's and my friendship in that way was really touching. I honestly didn't know I meant so much to him. I didn't know what to say.

Once it soaked in, what he was offering seemed impossible to accept.

"But I-I don't even know anything about doing injections, not like Lonzi," I replied.

"Don't worry. I'll teach you what you need to know, and I'll even vouch for you," Rick told me.

Honey, I wasn't too sure if that's what I wanted to do. "Umm, let me think about it and get back with you."

"I'll be waiting on that call," Rick said.

I went home and thought about everything. So many emotions swirled around in my head. I was excited, nervous, and scared, all balled up into one big emotion. I called him a few days later and told him I wanted to do it.

Rick explained that whenever people called and wanted to get work done, he'd refer them to me. We made an agreement that I would continue to get the silicone from him because the doctor that Lonzi got the medicine from wouldn't meet anyone else. He had too much to lose. People were so desperate to get their butts done, I found out quickly that it didn't even matter that they had never heard of Kimberly Smedley. They were just happy to know that someone was taking over Lonzi's business.

Almost all of Lonzi's clients were either in Atlanta or Detroit. Naturally, those would be the two main cities I worked in. Detroit and Atlanta had so many strippers, and all of them wanted to be at the top of their game.

It took about a month for the phone to start ringing. I remember the first time someone called. I was so nervous. This was all new to me, and Lonzi was no longer here to guide me. This was all on me, honey, so I had to be on point.

Rather than make trips out of town over and over, I told each person that I would call them a few days before I'd be in their city. I waited until I had my first ten clients before making the trip. It made more sense that way.

In the beginning, most clients who called me were transsexuals. I wasn't sure how they would react to me, because I wasn't anything like Lonzi. Also, there were a lot of things to be concerned about.

First of all, let's not forget that this was an illegal cash business. Getting robbed was a real possibility, so I had to be extra careful. I also had to be cautious because many of the transsexual clients had AIDS or HIV. That was serious, honey, so I had to take serious precautions. That was one on-the-job risk I was not willing to take.

Detroit was especially risky because getting robbed was as prevalent as going to get gas. Even after weighing all the possible issues, I still felt this was something I really needed to do.

The salon had slowed down tremendously, and my boys were in private school. I wanted them to get the best education possible, so taking them out wasn't an option. The extra money I could make from doing injections would really help me with their tuition since I was doing it solo.

Standing on my feet all day at the salon started to get old. I developed fibroid tumors, and hemorrhaged so bad just from standing up. It wouldn't even be time for my cycle. Yet, there I was like a faucet. Yes, honey, it was definitely time for a change, and to make some extra money.

About three weeks later, I called *my clients* to let them know where I would be and when I would arrive. I wasn't even sure if anyone would show up. Lonzi had some big shoes to fill, chile. Literally. I could only hope I would get the same respect.

When I arrived at the hotel and went up to my room, there wasn't a soul lined up outside my door waiting. That's the opposite of what I was used to seeing whenever I tagged along with Lonzi. I started to feel like I wasted my time. Then about an hour later, my first client finally showed up.

Honey, my first client was a transvestite! I was so nervous. She was beautiful. To my surprise, she didn't want her butt done, she wanted her breasts done.

At least I'd done a few butt injections that time when Lonzi was sick, so I had a little practice, but I'd never done anyone's breasts. Now, I'd seen Lonzi do it a few times, so I tried my best to remember exactly what I saw. To be honest, I didn't know how in the world I was going to pull it off.

All I remembered was that I had to inject into the muscle and be extremely careful because it was close to the lungs. Baay-bee, let me tell you . . . trying to get that little needle through that thick muscle was something else, honey. I had to use strength that I never even knew I had.

Men are built different than women. They have significantly more muscle mass, and they definitely don't have much fat on their chest either. Not even the out of shape ones. Their chest is an extremely dense place. In other words, it's hard as hell.

Usually, men who wanted breasts would take steps to soften their chest muscle. I discovered they took hormones to loosen up that density. If they didn't, it was difficult to inject them. It was like pushing the needle through solid rock! I couldn't even understand how Lonzi did it.

Now, don't get it twisted, I don't have anything against transvestites. Some of my closest friends are gay. However, I had some reservations about making breasts on a man, and I didn't feel right morally. It wasn't sitting well with me.

On this particular trip, most of the clients were transvestites. Some of them weren't first timers either. They knew Lonzi and had, had work done before. I always felt good about making people feel beautiful. That's why I loved doing hair. But if I didn't feel right about something, I felt there was a higher chance that I might mess it up.

Some of them did want their butts done, but majority wanted breasts. I worked my way through each client, and they all seemed to be satisfied. Chile, I had to put my legs, back, and arms into that work. Maybe there was a better way to do it; I didn't know. It's crazy, but I had zero medical training, and the clients were more than patient with me. Some even said my work was better!

Before injecting each client, I said a silent prayer. "Lord, please don't let me mess any one of these people up." They all were nice and trusted me to do a good job. So far, to this date, I never got any complaints.

The very next morning, I left Detroit and flew back home and fell into a deep sleep. When I woke up that late afternoon and tried to sit up, severe pain shot through my core. Something was wrong. My chest hurt so bad, I had to remain in bed due to the pain. It felt like I had cracked a rib or something.

I ended up going to the doctor and learned I had severe muscle strain. I pulled a muscle in my chest while trying to inject the silicone into the client's chest. Yes, it was that dang on hard that I strained and hurt myself. It took a couple more trips of me enduring that same pain before I quit doing transvestites. The recuperation was just too long. I figured it was a sign I shouldn't be doing that anyway. From that point on, I would only accept female clients.

Soon after, I stopped doing breasts altogether because after doing some research I learned it was not safe. The risk of it going into the lungs was much greater, along with other risks.

It was somewhat of a loss though. I must say, the transvestites in Detroit treated me very well. I have much respect for them. Even now, I still have a lot of gay friends in the "D," and I still frequent the drag queen shows. My straight friends call me a fag hag, but I don't care. I just love it!

During that time, my life began to change and word spread that I was in business. I can't even complain about the money I made. I was making so much money that I came to realize how little Lonzi paid me when I assisted him in Detroit. It's okay though, because the saying "it gets greater later," stands true. It definitely did.

Chapter 10

Disclosure

It is no secret the injections Lonzi gave me changed the way I felt about myself considerably. I can definitely admit that. Guys were attracted to me before, but having a firm, round booty added a whole new set of admirers to the table. I'd be walking down the street before my surgery, and a guy or two might say "hello" and try to make small talk. But when I walked down the street after I got my butt done, honey, it was a completely different thing.

"Damn, baby, you lookin' good!"

"Baby, I can't *not* talk to you. You are sexy as hell."

"Can I buy you a house? A car? Anything?" Sometimes, it would be hilarious. I mean, the men would be so funny, the way they were coming with all their game. I don't know what it is about butts that make men go crazy, but oh, they do.

And ethnicity didn't matter one iota. Black guys, of course, loved it. But even white, Hispanic, as well as Asian men would be breaking their necks to see a sista walk away, swaying her thick hips. I always laughed to myself when I thought about it. I enjoyed the attention because it was new.

Because of those personal experiences, I am under the impression that most men prefer a woman with curves.

For the most part, I can understand why some women want to be skinny. Especially for those who model or work in the movie industry or are on TV. But let me tell you something: men really do love some cushion for the pushin', honey. It's sexy to have a bit of meat on those bones. Like grandma used to say, "Even a dog wants a bone with some meat on it." These were the kinds of conversations that often took place while I was working on my clients.

Incidentally, my table side manner (no pun intended) and great rapport with those same women led them to feel comfortable enough to ask me questions about sex. They wanted to know if it felt different before and after the injections.

"Does it go to your va-jay-jay?"

"Absolutely not!" I laughed.

"Do you still have feeling in your butt afterward?"

"Yes, my dear, it feels natural, as if it were your own."

"Does it make anal sex hurt less?"

"Anal sex has nothing to do with your butt having injections. It may just give him a   little something more to hold on to," I answered.

The first time I heard some of these questions, I was thinking, *Now what kind of questions are these?* But honestly, the dumb questions are the ones not asked. I started to answer from my own standpoint. Then I thought about it and figured I'd ask other clients their opinion, since my answers were based on my own personal experiences. Some of them shared their experiences with me.

One girl told me sex with her boyfriend before her shots was very routine. He would always get on top of her. They would do their thing in that position, and then she would get on top of him. And then, the grand finale was a doggy-style position. After she got butt shots from me, baaay-beee . . . she told me she wasn't expecting her sex life to transform the way it did. When she walked around naked before she got the enhancements, her man didn't really react. However, after the butt shots, she said if he could even barely see through her pajamas, he was on her like white on rice. He was willing to try new things and had even become more romantic. He'd be massaging her butt and taking his time in a whole new way. She loved it and the sex was great.

Yes, I could definitely relate to her experience. My sex life was always good. I never had a problem in that department. Things did get spicier after my injections, too. I felt so much more comfortable in my skin afterward. I felt more sexually appealing, and that certainly increased my confidence. I felt like I could twerk it for real, honey.

Like some of my satisfied clients, I too, had put my new rump shaker to the test. I used to have my stripper clients teaching me things, and I had a lot of fun trying them out. I would clap it, pop it, and drop it, baby. Now, I'm saving all of that for that special someone.

From time to time, women have also asked whether they should disclose the fact they have had work done. I think it's totally up to the individual. The good thing about shots is that nobody has to know if you don't tell them. Even some celebrities have done x-rays trying to prove they haven't had any butt enhancements. Enhancements won't show up on an x-ray unless you have implants. If you are with a man who you are comfortable with and feel compelled to tell him, then go ahead. However, I feel that is your private business, and it's perfectly fine to keep it to yourself. One of my clients still wishes she had done just that.

She had her butt done about eight months before she met her boyfriend. She never mentioned anything to him about it. One night they were having pillow talk, and she decided to tell him.

Ever since she let him know, he never ceased bringing it up. He talked about it all the time, and it made her feel very uncomfortable. I could only imagine how annoying that must have been. For example, say you wore a wig and of course you knew it was a wig, but that didn't mean you wanted somebody else to keep saying, "Girl, that's a wig you're wearing." It took away from the beauty of it, no matter how good it looked.

When she came back to me to get her second set of injections, she told me they were no longer together. She left him and I didn't blame her. She said all the way down to the last seconds of their relationship, when she was walking out the door, he was still yelling some mean things to her. He said, "Good! Go! You and your fake ass can get up outta' here!" She was still a little upset, so I tried my best not to burst into laughter. But I didn't try hard enough, because the next thing I knew, I had tears in my eyes and I couldn't breathe because I was cracking up.

"That's not funny, Miss Kim!" she said to me.

"I know, I know, I'm sorry. Next time I bet you'll know to keep your damn mouth shut!" She couldn't deny that I was right, and we had a good laugh together.

Chapter 11

For All the Wrong Reasons

I didn't judge any of my clients. They all had their reasons for getting the procedure done. It didn't matter their background. It didn't matter where they were from. All that mattered was they wanted to change something about themselves. That's why people sought me out.

I knew one thing for sure, as a human being and a woman, it was natural for us to want to conform to the people around us. The folks who walk around who don't conform to what other people think are definitely special. As a matter of fact, they are to be admired.

But to be equally admired are those who are brave enough to take steps to be who they want to be. As long as you are not encroaching your ideas and thoughts on another person's life, go ahead, pursue your happiness. I like to say, "Do you."

When you do something that makes you feel good about yourself, honey, you start pulling courage and strength to do things you wouldn't normally do. That man who has been abusing you either physically or verbally, suddenly has no more power over you. You start to love yourself so deeply that anything or anyone who tries to interfere with that gets cut off. I believe it has something to do with self-esteem.

It may seem strange, but many people suddenly want a new wardrobe to match that new look. They may want a new love to match that new physique. They want a new car to show off now that they have new self-confidence. They have a new desire for life because they feel like a new person. And baby, ain't nothing wrong with that, as long as it's done for yourself.

For me to play a role in any part of that, made me feel comfortable about what I was doing, despite its illegal nature.

I use the term illegal lightly. Let me explain. The law books in the country define the term illegal in several ways. The first being: an act that is not authorized by law. But my case was considered as something outside the sphere of law, not classifiable as being either legal or illegal.

When I was charged for doing the injections, it wasn't worded how you would expect. My actual charge was "conspiracy to commit interstate commerce of a mislabeled, misbranded device." There were no laws specifically banning the use of silicone injected into the buttocks.

In 1965, the FDA banned silicone injections for doctors without a special permit. But all other specifics deal with the breasts. It was later banned from being injected directly into the breast tissue. Well, I injected men with silicone in their chest muscles, and there was also nothing on the books about injecting into the glutes (butt). I'm not advocating what I was doing. I'm simply stating the facts as they were at the time.

I believe the attention my case brought to this underground phenomenon, actually sparked law writers to specify exactly what is and isn't allowed. In other words, new laws are being written right now.

Outside of the U.S., in some countries, butt injections are not illegal. It is viewed as a "do at your own risk" procedure. Some countries such as the Dominican Republic and other Caribbean places don't mention it at all.

I must say I have had some very interesting clients from all over the world and from all walks of life. I've had doctors, nurses, lawyers, real estate agents, computer analyst, strippers, athletes' wives, singers, dancers, actors and actresses, so many celebrities, honey. They all came for one thing, and that was to enhance their butts. Each person had their own reason, and I always wanted to know more.

The first question I always asked was why they wanted to have their butts done. Some of them said they'd always wanted a larger bottom or wider hips. Others said they were inspired by Serena Williams or Jennifer Lopez. I just wanted to make sure they weren't doing it for the wrong reasons.

One client in particular wanted her butt and hips done. She said she was scheduled to have breast implants the following month. The lady wasn't smiling and didn't seem as anxious as many other clients. I sensed that something was wrong. I didn't want to pry too much, but in a very respectful way I asked her why she wanted so much done.

She began crying. Honey, she cried as though she'd been holding her tears in forever and finally let them break free. I'd seen tears of joy, and I'd seen tears from the pain caused by the actual injections, but never like this, right before a procedure. I just embraced her and let her cry. I gave her some time to get herself together before I asked her to explain what was wrong.

"My man keeps cheating on me. He messes with all these girls with big butts. I want one too, so maybe he'll be faithful to me."

I knew right after that, that I could not perform the procedure. She wasn't getting it because of her own desires. My client didn't want to recreate herself. She wanted to recreate him, and that was a big difference.

"Sweetheart," I said. "You don't need a new butt; you need a new boyfriend." She looked up at me and said the saddest thing.

"But I won't ever find another man like him."

"Girl, please!" I said, almost yelling at the poor woman. "He sounds like a dog, and baby, trust me; there is no shortage of dogs on this earth. This procedure is something you do for you because you have to live with it, and although many of us do it to look good for the men, we still have lots of joy about it. At the end of the day you have to be happy. The last thing you need to be worried about is trying to do it to please some disrespectful man. You don't seem happy at all." She tried to reason with me, but I wasn't having it. She even told me she would pay me whatever I wanted.

"No ma'am. It isn't even about the money. I want my clients to feel good about what they have done."

"Well, I'll be happier afterward," she said in response.

"Yeah, until he cheats again, and then you'll be trying to find something else. What will it be next, drugs? Girl, go home and get right with yourself," I said to her. All this time I didn't realize I was pointing my finger like a mother scolding her child.

She wasn't trying to hear me at first, but I finally talked some sense into her. Although I may have been doing something illegal, I still had a strong set of moral codes I followed. I just couldn't put my signature on something that didn't feel right.

About six months later, I received a call from her telling me that she found out her boyfriend was bisexual, and he left her for another man. That's right, A MAN. She thanked me for talking some sense into her.

I smiled and said, "Anytime."

I ended the call shaking my head because some things we just couldn't compete with, and that was definitely one of them.

Chapter 12

When it Rains it Pours

Six months after my first job, I was now known to most as Miss Kim. My client base had grown tremendously. Honey, I was now doing many strippers and magazine models. Business was great and my personal life wasn't too bad either. I'd met this really nice guy, and we had been dating for a while. I was traveling all over the country, and I happened to meet him in Arkansas. That's right, I said Arkansas.

Cedric became a big part of my life and my kids' life. He spoiled me, and it helped that the kids really liked him too. One day he asked me to marry him. I wasn't really sure if I wanted to get married. I had a lot going on. After I thought long and hard about it, I finally accepted his proposal.

Men like him were rare. I can distinctly remember when I'd be working, gone for days. I'd come home late and find a hot bath already waiting. I wouldn't have to cook because he had already made the kids dinner, so I could relax. He would even get up and take them to school in the morning so I could sleep in. He didn't spoil me in terms of giving me much money; he actually didn't have much. That, however, didn't matter because I was making plenty of money on my own. Money wasn't an issue for me. As a matter of fact, I was making more money than I ever had. The first thing I did was upgrade my house. I bought a bigger, nicer house in a better neighborhood. My kids had a basketball court in the backyard. It felt good. I even enrolled them in public school. The schools in the area where we moved were much better.

My friend Eric's words played over and over in my head. "Quick money goes quick! You better do something with that money, girl." That's what he used to say when I worked at the shop, and he would see me blowing the money my son's father would give me. Eric used to buy and sell properties, and he wanted me to go in with him. I not only decided to go in with him in the housing game, but I agreed that we should do it and step our game up altogether. I had a decent amount of money saved up, and I was ready to do some big things, honey.

We decided to build houses. Eric had always been a go getter ever since I'd known him. I felt he'd be a good partner, especially since I knew he had already been successful. He was very familiar with the real estate market. This was a good thing because I knew we could make a lot of money, legally. It was something I didn't have to hide and I could feel proud about.

We built our first house and it felt so good. I can barely describe it. The experience was phenomenal! Although it was just a little starter house, it felt like we built a mansion. Just to know that I did something so productive made me feel wonderful inside. Don't get me wrong, I enjoyed making people feel good by doing enhancements, too. All my clients generally felt better about themselves after the procedure. But at the end of the day, it was still illegal. I only started doing injections because I needed extra money. I definitely needed it because I had so many bills and two boys to take care of. However, if I could make good money legally, why not? In my younger years I'd had a few run-ins with the law. Believe me, I had no desire to ever deal with that again.

I really got into the business of building houses and took it serious. So serious that I stopped doing butt enhancements. That's right, I went cold turkey and became a full-time real estate investor. Everything was going as planned. Better actually. Houses were selling left and right. I couldn't get them built fast enough. I envisioned creating a real-estate empire, one house at a time. Then suddenly, the worst happened. The housing market crashed. Everybody was in a panic. Houses stopped moving and the bubble burst. This was not good for me. It wasn't good for Eric. It was bad for the whole country.

Honey, when it rains it pours. At the same time that all of that was happening, things at home started to go south as well. My relationship with my fiancé began to crumble. His money started getting really low, and chile, you know how men can be when their money is funny. He already didn't have much to begin with, and this really put him into a downward spiral.

Cedric was paying all the bills. He knew I had my own money, but he still insisted on paying for everything. I never asked him to do that, but he insisted. Hey, I wasn't going to refuse him. I was raised to believe that a man is supposed to be the head of the house and take care of everything. I definitely did not want him to feel like less of a man, so I let him do as he desired.

You see, he left Arkansas and moved to Atlanta to be with me. He came with his life savings and hadn't been working for at least six months. How he thought he could live off those minimal funds without securing a job is beyond me. All of his money ran out pretty quickly, and he started saying it was my fault! Damn . . . really! People can be very crazy, and I saw it firsthand.

Of course, because of his anger, the cheating started. He was always mad, always upset about every little thing. Let's see, we've got a man who is constantly miserable, broke, and now cheating? Oh hell to the no, baby! That wasn't about to be my life. He had to go. So we ended it. I have a very low tolerance for bull crap.

I felt I had no choice in the matter of making sure my household remained intact. So I had to get back to what I knew.

Injections. It had been awhile since I went out of town to do butt injections, but that phone of mine had never stopped ringing off the hook. It was going non-stop. I kept turning people down because I was focused on the housing business. I developed a passion for it, and I wished I could've kept on doing it. I just wasn't going to beat a dead horse. I had mouths to feed and plenty of bills to pay. Talk about thinking irrationally at the time.

Even though I was just starting back up, I was crazy busy. When I told clients I couldn't make it to their particular location, they were on a plane, bus, or train to see me in Atlanta. I even got a little spoiled having clients come to me. It allowed me to stay home a little more, and I loved it because I could spend more time with my boys. But that situation wasn't realistic if I wanted to stay relevant in the business. Some of my clients and potential clients began going to other people, and some of them were getting disfigured and sick. Some were just getting too much and were looking ridiculous. I couldn't let them do that to themselves. It just wasn't right.

After about four months, I decided to get back out on the road. Usually, I'd wait until I had enough people requesting injections in the same city before I went. I got a phone call from this lady I knew from Atlanta named Pam. She moved out of town, but called me requesting that I come and see her. She happened to be not too far from where I was staying during my trip, so I told her that she could stop by my hotel.

When I got there, Pam called me and asked if she could come the next day. I was ready to go home, but since I knew her, I reluctantly agreed.

She arrived at my hotel around ten in the morning. When she finally showed up to my room, I had two other clients there. Pam seemed so anxious. She kept looking down at her phone and looking around. I was used to clients being really nervous about the procedure when it was their first time, but Pam was no newbie to shots. I'd worked on her before, so I wondered why she was acting so strange. Honey, she was as fidgety as ever.

While I serviced the two other clients, she got up and said she'd be right back. She needed to run down to her car. I worked diligently on the clients and sent them on their way. When Pam came back up, I got started on her. The whole time she was getting her injections, something felt off. There was an unsettling energy in the room. At that time I couldn't put my finger on it, but I could feel that something wasn't right.

After we were done, Pam didn't leave right away. She kind of just hung around, sitting on the couch looking at her phone. We made small talk and chatted. After about fifteen minutes, there was a loud knock at the door. Pam jumped up and headed to the door, and that really caught me off guard. *Why would she be jumping up?* I thought. I instantly got pissed because all of my clients knew my rules. I did not allow clients to ever get up to open the door, and Pam knew this, so her jumping up angered me and alerted me to the fact that she must have been expecting company.

As she headed toward the door, I yelled out "PAM!" but I was too late.

A man and a woman burst through the door holding guns. My heart rate went into overdrive. I couldn't believe this was happening.

"Get on the floor! Everybody on the floor NOW! We're from vice squad!"

"When are the police coming?" I asked repeatedly, because they didn't have on uniforms. And even if they were from vice squad, uniformed officers would show up as back up.

"Shut-up! Shut-up!" they kept telling me. Something told me they were not really the police. Another give away was the young lady. I had the type of memory that never forgot a face. I knew her from somewhere. She looked so familiar to me. I just couldn't recall it at the moment.

Later, it came to me that the female was Pam's daughter! I remembered her face because she had accompanied Pam to Atlanta once, on one of her trips to see me. But it didn't come to me then. It wasn't until much later, after they came in that I was able to really confirm that they were not police at all. I knew that business was risky, but damn! This was a whole different level of dangerous. This was some straight bullshit!

Those perpetrators tied Pam's and my hands behind our backs with some heavy duty trash bag ties. "Where's the money? Where's the money?" they kept asking. I wasn't telling them anything. I just kept quiet and hoped to God they wouldn't find it.

Unfortunately, they did. They found the money stashed in the nightstand in the bedroom. I was in a suite, and the bedroom was in a different area. When they finally left, Pam tried to act like she was traumatized. She tried to leave, but I had already figured out that this wasn't random. Although at the time I didn't realize the girl was Pam's daughter, I had an undeniable feeling that somehow Pam was involved and had set me up.

I don't know who Pam thought she was dealing with, but I told her she better sit down because I was going to kick her ass if she didn't get me my money back.

"I don't know what you are talking about," she said.

"You know damn well what I am talking about, and if you don't give me my money back I guarantee you will wish you had." She trembled with fear, because I was all up in her face. Before I knew it I wrapped my hands around her neck, trying to choke the shit out of her. I was furious.

"Please let go of my neck, I can't breathe," she eked out. The anger bubbling up inside me allowed me to squeeze a little tighter. Finally, I slammed her up against the wall.

As I held her against the wall, I thought about what I was going to do. It took a minute, but I finally let her go. I went through her purse and found her wallet until I found her driver's license. I took it out of the wallet and stuck it in my bra.

"I'm taking this as security until I get my damn money back."

"Kim, I promise I don't know who that was."

"Bitch, that was your daughter. I remember meeting her at your sister's house. I want my thirty thousand dollars back!" I spat.

Really, I was plotting. I made about thirteen thousand dollars. But I knew if I told her it was thirty, and once they gave her, her cut, she was going look at them like they were crazy, thinking they cheated her. For a moment I felt a little satisfaction. I knew how money could destroy a relationship. I was there going through it.

"Get your shit and get out! I will deal with you later. Trust me, you haven't seen the last of me," I threatened.

She grabbed her things and ran out of the room. I sat down and cried. I was so heated.

The monetary loss I took from the robbery was nowhere near as severe as the violation I felt in my core from being held against my will. When somebody does that to you, it takes something from you. The helplessness becomes like some type of torture. If I could, I would have kept Pam in that room longer, but I figured it was safer to get out of there. I had illegal silicone in my possession, and I didn't know what those fools might do next.

Nevertheless, I couldn't just let it go. I called one of the pimps I knew that would often bring his girls to me. He got right on it and asked how I wanted to deal with the situation. I told him I'd get back to him. For a while I thought about getting her back, but after I got over the initial shock, I started thinking rationally. I prayed about it, and then I decided to just let it go. It was a loss, but I had to charge it to the game.

A few years later, I learned from a client that Pam had passed away from a tumor. All I could say was, "WOW!" I was learning quickly that I couldn't trust anyone. From that day forward, I promised myself I would handle my business in a totally different way.

Chapter 13

A Sign and a Sacrifice

By 2002, I'd been in business for quite some time. Things had been going pretty good for me. The only problem I had was my availability being so limited, and I didn't get to spend as much time with my kids as I liked. It was difficult to sit still. About three years had passed since I first got started.

In December of 2002, I received a phone call. Honey, let me tell you, it was a phone call that changed my life completely. I'll never forget it. It was on a Sunday morning when my telephone rang. No matter how much I traveled, I always made it my business to be home on the weekends, especially Sunday, so we could go to church as a family.

When I answered the phone, I was very surprised that this particular lady was even calling me. We weren't exactly friends. I knew her through a friend of mine, who fathered two of her children. He was in prison serving a nine year sentence. I hadn't heard from him in about four years, so the fact that his baby mama was calling me was a little strange. When she spoke, I could hear the trembling in her voice. I didn't know what was up, but I could tell something wasn't right. KaSandra seemed very upset. She asked if I would please stop by and bring her and the kids some food because they were all hungry. At the time she *only* had seven kids.

I wasn't that surprised, because I'd heard since her man (my friend) had gone to prison, she fell on some really hard times. She'd been using drugs for a while, and we all know that drugs can make any unfortunate situation worse. I felt bad for her, and I really felt bad for the children. They are so innocent.

KaSandra struggled with drug abuse for many years. My friend, well he had tried on several occasions to put her in rehab. He wanted her to get clean. She would go in and come back like she'd beat the disease, but shortly after she'd relapse and start using all over again. It was just an overall sad story.

After my sons and I left church, we went to the grocery store. I picked up some eggs, milk, juice, meat, cereal, rice and whatever else I could think of that they might need. We took everything to her house, and we were happy to do so. I had always instilled in my kids the importance of helping others when they had a need in their lives. When we got there, the kids were playing outside. They were all young. I asked them where their mom was. They pointed to the door and said she was inside.

I knocked on the door and she let me in. The apartment was a mess. Just dirty. She had a pit bull running around inside. Immediately when I opened the door, that dog smell hit me like a ton a bricks. It wasn't a good environment for children. There was poop on the floor and everything. Honey, I just stepped on over it and went to the kitchen so I could drop off the groceries. The whole time I was just shaking my head.

After the bags were put up, I went into the living room to sit and talk to her. I noticed a car seat sitting on the floor. Inside was the cutest little caramel baby girl. She was just too adorable.

"How old is she?" I asked.

"Four months old," KaSandra answered.

"She's so adorable. What's her name?" I asked.

"That's . . ." she said, not looking me in the eyes.

When I picked her up she started bouncing in my arms, smiling from ear to ear and cooing. As I continued to play with the baby, out of the blue, KaSandra asked me the craziest question.

"You mind keeping her for about six months?"

"What! Excuse me?" I replied, thinking I hadn't heard her right.

"Look, I gotta go back to prison. My family is gon' take the other children, but don't nobody want the baby," she explained.

According to KaSandra, the prison let her come home just to have the baby.

"So, will you take her?" she asked again.

"No! I'm sorry. I can't," I immediately told her. There was no way, honey. Chile, please! I wasn't trying to take on that type of responsibility. My kids were now ten and sixteen, and I was not ready for any more. No thank you. I was done with the whole baby thing a long time ago. What in the world would I do with a baby? No ma'am. Not Miss Kim. Un-unn.

"If no one takes her I'm a have to put her in a foster home," she explained.

"Where is the baby's daddy? Why can't he keep his child?" I asked.

"Girl, he is in prison and his family won't take her."

I shook my head. I felt really terrible about her situation, but oh well, honey. There was no *way* I was taking that responsibility on. It was not going to happen.

The baby was cute though. She had the most precious little face, but I wasn't sure if the baby had any health problems or other issues. After all, her mom was a drug addict and the odds of her being born with something wrong were pretty high. I left KaSandra and the children there with the groceries and my prayers and I went home.

That night, I continuously tossed and turned. I couldn't get that baby off my mind, no matter how hard I tried. For two whole days I thought about her non-stop. I went to sleep and even dreamed about her. I could see her pretty face as vivid as if it were painted on a colorful pallet. I couldn't deny it or act like I didn't see that dreaming about her was a sign from God. He was telling me that she needed me. Maybe I needed her.

KaSandra kept calling and asking me to take her. She was blowing up my phone non-stop and left me multiple voice mails. "Please come and get my baby. Please!" I made up my mind, I was going to get Lil' Miss Keron.

Before I took her home with me, I made her mother accompany me to the pediatrician. Honey, she was four months old and had never been to the doctor's office. To me, that was unacceptable. Her mother had not taken her for any medical follow-ups since the day she was born. She hadn't been immunized or anything. Oh yes, this baby really needed me.

This poor child wasn't even on any type of baby formula, and no, she wasn't getting breast fed either. Keron had been on whole milk since birth. Her little fragile stomach must have been cramping something terrible. I just couldn't imagine.

After the trip to the pediatrician, we immediately had guardianship papers drawn up. We then had them notarized to make it somewhat official. It was all very basic, nothing too formal since this was only going to be temporary. While incarcerated, her mom would detoxify, and by the time she got out, she could provide for her and the rest of her children in a much better fashion. After doing all of this, the idea of having Keron started to grow on me.

I was actually excited to bring her home. My mom was at my house when I walked in with the baby.

The Backside of the Story

"Whose baby is that?" was the first thing my mother asked.

"Her name is Keron, and I'm going to be keeping her for a while." Mom looked at me as though I had ten heads.

"What's a while? Chile . . . what in the world are you going to do with a baby?"

"Don't worry. I'll make it work," I replied.

"Kim, please! Girl, you ain't got time for no baby. You're already always gone out of town. How is this gonna work?"

I didn't respond to my mother because I knew she was right. What was I going to do with a baby? I didn't have the slightest clue. All I knew was that I was led by a greater force, a higher power to take her. And I did. It was a sacrifice, but I wouldn't change it for anything in the world.

When her mom came home, she was in worse shape than when she went in. The baby stayed with me. Today, she is eleven years old. I am her mom in every way a woman can be a great mother to a child. My sons are her brothers, and we all love her dearly.

Over the years, her mom has taken me to court in an attempt to get her back. I would have loved for her to be with her birth mom, but she won't get off the drugs. What kind of person would I be to put her back in that type of environment? I couldn't leave her with her mother. It wasn't safe.

I have never kept her from knowing that side of her family, and I never will. It's important to me and important for her. Keron and her siblings never asked for the situation they were born into. Since she has so many siblings, I wanted her to know them because there is nothing like having a relationship with your family. But it's my job to protect her because she is my daughter.

Of all her siblings, Keron was the only one born without any drugs in her system. Her mom was pregnant while in prison, so her system remained clean. My baby got lucky. I don't know, and we will never know, but prison may have saved my daughter's life. I am so thankful for Keron. She is smart and healthy.

I feel so blessed to have her. If I never find my true purpose in life, I know she was part of it. Occasionally, I think about my mom's reaction and how she thought I was stone crazy at first for bringing this beautiful child home. But now . . . lawd, I don't know what my mom would do, or where she would be without her. She loves that little girl, her granddaughter.

Now, I can't even picture my life without my daughter, and neither can my mother, nor anyone else in my family. I honestly believe my mom is so connected to Keron because of the issues my mom had when she was younger. Her biological mom had also given her up because of her addiction to alcohol. I believe Mom and Keron share a special connection, which is one of the reasons they are so close. My boys, since the day I brought her home, have never had a problem with her being in our family. She is their little sister, and they are very protective of her.

Keron is child number seven. I know that seven is the number of completion. She has definitely completed my life. She is my silver lining. In all the wrong that I have done in my life, she is my personal testimony that I have some degree of good in me too.

Chapter 14

For Your Information

So what is silicone anyway? I am far from a scientist or doctor. I don't have any medical training, but I can try my best to explain it to you.

Silicon (without the 'e') can be found on the periodic table. You remember the periodic table, don't you? From high school chemistry? It lists the known elements. Well, I never paid it much attention, and I had no idea I'd be dealing with anything related to chemistry back then.

Anyway, silicone is a polymer of silicon. A polymer is a version of the original thing. So in this case, silicone is a version of silicon after several chemical processes take place. It can be in liquid, solid, or gel forms.

According to *Stedman's Medical Dictionary*, 26th Edition, approximately two million women in the United States alone have had breast implants since the 1960s. Silicone was widely used in all kinds of surgical implants, including tubes and other products, not just for cosmetic purposes.

In 1992, silicone was banned by the Food and Drug Administration (FDA), because of issues caused by leakage. However, the breasts and butt are very different in anatomy, and there have been few studies done on the effects of silicone injected into the buttocks.

Occasionally I've seen horror stories of migration, where the silicone traveled to other locations in the body, other than where it was originally injected. Sometimes there is severe lumping because the silicone has clumped up and deformed someone's backside. In my experience, that hasn't been something I've seen often. Fortunately, none of my clients have ever reported such incidents happening.

However, when these things happened to people, it was very difficult to find a surgeon who would remove the silicone. There were a few out there, and luckily, as my clientele grew, I was able to come into contact with some very amazing people.

I had a client who wanted me to meet a doctor. The doctor practiced in New York, and she was very talented and specialized in body sculpting. My client explained that networking with the doctor would be a good connection for me because this doctor had worked on some women and transsexuals who had gotten injections and the outcome was horrific. The injections had given them major problems and they needed help.

Most cosmetic surgeons wouldn't touch a person with silicone injections. Mostly because they were afraid of doing even more damage. No doctor wanted to risk being the cause of any type of permanent disfiguration.

However, this doctor felt it was necessary to help people who were suffering. She would remove as much of the silicone as she could, using her special technique. She was able to do it with as little damage as possible. The problem wasn't so much with the butts as it was with the silicone in people's faces. Most of the time, the worst issues occurred in that specific area.

The majority of doctors who don't touch botched silicone injection jobs in the United States, choose not to, not only because they don't want to cause more damage, but because silicone removal is completely unfamiliar. Silicone injections in the U.S. are illegal. And therefore, most US doctors aren't trained in any removal techniques.

People who have come to me with these types of issues are oftentimes desperate. I've had to refer some clients to doctors in other parts of the world, such as Mexico, the Dominican Republic, and even Colombia. Doctors in these countries are much more familiar with silicone injections because the process is not illegal there. Silicone injection procedures are not governed by their law. There is nothing on their law books that regulate those types of surgeries. Because they are allowed to do injections, the removal process is something they are more familiar with as well.

There are always going to be procedures that are banned in the United States, but are legal in other countries. One example that comes to mind is the abortion pill. It had been approved in Europe years before the FDA approved it in the United States.

Honey, this country has a lot of red tape when it comes to getting medicines or procedures approved. The impatience many people experience while waiting for something to get approved, is what leads them to seek things out in the flourishing black markets of underground procedures.

There are many, many other examples. Millions of women suffer with unwanted facial hair. Those hairs are usually caused by too many male androgens or hormones floating around in the female body. There is nothing to correct this problem on the market, other than to deal with it externally by using lasers, razors, or electrolysis. All of these can burn the skin. However, in Europe, they actually have an approved medication, a pill you can take once a day that blocks the male hormones from wreaking havoc on the female body. It would stop the hair growth. What woman wants hair on her neck, chin, or chest?

This problem has a solution, but it is not available in the United States. The FDA has not approved that same pill currently available in Europe, here. I don't think the FDA always takes so long because they have malicious intent. Studies must be done to ensure that if I'm taking a pill to help my acne, I don't end up growing a third thumb. I do understand the requirements for approval. But I am not convinced that it's all about health and safety. I am almost positive there are plenty of politics and monetary issues involved as well.

During a conversation I had with the doctor out of New York, I explained what I was doing as far as the silicone injections, and I gave her every detail. She told me she was very familiar with those types of procedures because they were done in her home country all the time. She knew silicone injections were illegal here, but she also explained it was understudied and maybe the two of us could help one another out.

I believe more and more business began falling into my lap because of the honesty and integrity with which I operated. I was not like some of the other people doing injections just for the money and ignoring all other important factors. I actually would say, "No," if I thought what the client wanted was too risky. I turned people away if I suspected they weren't making their decision on their own. And most importantly, I had limits to the amount of silicone I was willing to inject. I genuinely cared.

Some of these black market prices were as cheap as $200 or $300, with no consideration to the damage it might cause to the recipient. Yes, it was illegal, and the customers knew their providers weren't medical professionals or licensed. But still, that wasn't an excuse to be overly reckless with what you were doing.

The doctor explained that many of her patients whom she removed silicone from, now had sagging skin. The skin's elasticity weakened once the fillers were removed. Especially in the face. She wanted to refer those people to me so I could fill in their sagging areas. In exchange, I could send clients to her that came to me wanting corrections.

I truly appreciated her thinking of me, but honey, there was no *way* on this planet that I was going to mess around with someone's face. Heck no! I was no plastic surgeon, and I wasn't going to pretend to be.

Previously, I had seen how some people's faces looked after getting injections, and believe me, it looked horrible. That was big in the transvestite world. I knew for sure that I wanted absolutely no parts of that. Thanks, but no thanks.

I understood people wanting butt injections, because there was no such surgery available in the United States that could produce the same results. At least nothing legal. But facelifts and other reconstructive surgeries that changed the face were commonplace now. There was no need to take on the risk of doing a black market procedure, when you could get something done by a board certified surgeon. One thing that holds true is: you get what you pay for. I was definitely staying away from certain body parts.

In Detroit I had a client who wanted to bring her boyfriend, a male stripper, to see me. I asked her why he wanted to see me and if he was gay. She assured me he wasn't. For the life of me, I couldn't figure out what I could possibly do for a straight man. Even if he was a stripper, I couldn't imagine why he would want to make his butt bigger.

The true reason he wanted to see me was a real shocker. We met up in a hotel room, and not long after introductions were made, this girl's boyfriend whipped out his penis! I jumped back. I couldn't believe it. He wanted silicone injections in his penis to make it bigger. It wasn't the first time I had ever heard of such a thing, but that was surely the first time I had been asked to do it.

Lonzi used to do it. Honey, I honestly think he just enjoyed touching other men's private parts.

I simply told them it was something I did not do. A penis has a main vein that runs through it, and I didn't feel comfortable taking that kind of chance. I referred him to a drag queen I knew who only worked on men and was more familiar with that type of procedure. But he declined the offer and insisted I do it because he didn't want another man touching his penis.

Unfortunately, I didn't know any other females who could do it. He was very disappointed. But I guess he wasn't as disappointed as he was desperate, because he eventually gave in and had it done by some gay guy that another male dancer referred him to.

Injections into the penis didn't make it longer, it just made it fatter. He wanted it so bad, that he went through with it. There are actually some men walking around with silicone in their penis. So yes, ladies, we aren't the only ones that have issues with our bodies. Although I must admit, in my day, I've seen quite a few men who could have benefitted from those services. I certainly have.

Chapter 15

Super-Size Me

Everybody who owns a television knows the power of sex appeal. It oozes. Sex sells, and there is such a thing as the art of seduction, honey. Anybody trying to take their career to the next level knows that a sex symbol image can take you from zero to one hundred overnight.

This fact was obviously known by the well-respected, filthy rich management team in the Hip-Hop game. They came to me with this young lady who was a tomboy through and through. Her hair was plain, no fancy colors or anything like that. Her clothes were plain too. She dressed just like a boy. She was about to start her career as a rapper. This young lady could rap and she could sing too. A very talented young lady.

Someone from her management team called me and set up the appointment. At first, I was hesitant because I never took a client without confirming who referred them. Once I was able to establish the connection, I was okay with doing this young lady's butt shots. I was very private about my business for obvious reasons. Honey, you can never be too careful.

She flew out to Atlanta, and I went to their hotel. I can distinctly remember how nice the hotel was. I had to go up and meet her on the penthouse floor.

This young lady had a very sweet disposition. She had the softest, cutest voice. I remember looking at her little body and wondering, *What in the world am I gonna do with this chile?* They sure were prepared though. They showed me pictures of what their vision was for her. The look they were going for was very bootylicious and curvaceous. I knew it was going to be some work to get her to that point because it was hard for me to envision her that way. She was flat chested and skinny. But if anybody knows, I know that anything is possible.

I gave them the whole rundown and explained how the process worked and that we couldn't accomplish the look they wanted in just one session. They would have to come back. I would never inject too many cc's (cubic centimeters) of silicone in one session. There were too many risks involved. The clients who got the best results were the ones who had the most patience and went through the process of getting a butt slowly.

Butt injections hurt. There was no denying that. The whole time I was thinking, *This poor thing is gonna be hollering something terrible*! To my surprise, I was wrong. She took it like a soldier and endured the procedure like a champ.

She lay across the table and flinched with every poke, but overall she handled it well. The guy from her team who set up the appointment was referred to me by a stripper who danced in a well-known strip club in Miami. She told him that I was the go-to person.

"I hear you do the best work. That's why I entrusted her to you." That's what he told me. He was right too, because I was different than other people in the business. Most of my competition had all their clients' bodies looking generally the same. The injections were meant to enhance what the person already had. Injections beef you up, they are not meant to build you an entirely new body. There was only one way to totally reshape someone and that was with cosmetic surgery. Sometimes people get injections thinking it will change their entire figure.

Not really.

It can make a round butt rounder. A wide butt wider. But it couldn't transform a person 180 degrees. That was a common misconception many people had. I made all of that clear when dealing with my clients. The young lady I worked on only came to me that one time, but honey let me tell you, after that one session, there was nothing tomboy-like about her figure. Now her career is just like her backside . . . HUGE! I saw her not too long ago in Los Angeles at the BET Awards. I was backstage with a friend who worked for BET. The young lady was a huge star by now, and she was back there with her bodyguards. I looked at her and waved. She waved back, but then turned her head. Honey, please! That's why I never cared that much about celebrities. Baby, after they get what they want they act like they don't know the "Booty Lady."

Most of my clients were referred to me by strippers. People saw their bodies and wanted to look just like them. Sometimes people look down on strippers, but not me. They took their craft seriously and went to extreme measures to make sure they were successful.

They didn't get injections just to look good, but to be at the top of their game. Their bodies were a work of art, and many of them got paid top dollars for it. A bangin' body in the world of stripping was as important as books in the classroom. It was a necessity.

It didn't matter that they had done work to enhance themselves. I encouraged them to not go too big because it looked more natural. Even if their admirers knew, they still enjoyed their company and dropped plenty of money. With a super sexy look, they could rake in some serious dough.

Some of them were in school. Some of them were single mothers trying to make ends meet. Some ladies came to me with their rent money, wanting to get injections. They said it was okay because after the shots, they would make double or even triple what they were currently getting. And they were right. Something about a juicy, round booty caused men and women to seek them out. Dudes were paying to see it, and women were paying to get one.

Sometimes the ladies went a little overboard with the look they wanted. I would sit them down and explain they would make more money if their butt was a nice size and had a natural look to it. A super-booty that weighed more than the rest of their entire body was a dead give-away. In some cases, that could hurt more than it helped. The female rapper/singer I worked on was given the same advice. She was able to get a large butt because even though she was petite and tomboy looking, her hips matched her butt. She went a little larger than I would have suggested, but hey, that look has definitely worked for her.

The ones with the little chicken legs and a big ol' butt in the back looked the worst to me. Honey, I did this one celebrity who didn't take my advice. The amount she wanted was within a safe cc range, but in my opinion, it was still too much for her little chicken legs. She didn't care though; she said she wanted it anyway.

She had a singing career of her own back in the '90s, but she let that go in exchange for the family life. Now she's a managing mom and a very public supporter of her husband's career. You will find her at any one of his shows repping ATL. They are some very nice people too. The whole family. They are just as nice in real life as they are on television.

I don't regret doing her backside. I just wish she would have listened to me and kept it proportioned with her body. To me, hers is a definite dead give-away. I did her butt, but let me tell you, honey, I did not do anything to that face. She looked better in the face before she did anything to it.

The Backside of the Story

Getting butt injections is a decision that should be well thought out. Once it's done, it's done. There is no way to remove the silicone without major surgery, and most doctors in the United States will not touch it. Removal almost always causes severe scarring, lumping, or discoloration.

I simply didn't believe in overdoing it. It didn't look right to be a size two, with a butt that was a size ten. Many times I had to turn clients away. Some people were just too thirsty for real. I would ask them, "Sweetheart, what in the world are you going to do when you're fifty or sixty years old and you don't need all of that anymore?" Also, I told them, "Yes, it's cute now while you're using it to make money, but later on, chile, you are going to look a hot mess. Whatcha gonna do then?" That was not a concern of theirs. They lived in the now and were not worried about later.

That was the difference between my clients and me. No, I was not a doctor, a nurse, or any other type of medical professional. I didn't take any oaths or anything like that, but I couldn't have my name attached to any bad work. Not if I could help it. Besides, I knew some of these women were not thinking rationally. Some of them called me months later and thanked me for talking some sense into them.

Some ladies with a bigger butt agenda got mad at me for cutting them off from doing any more injections. Many times, they understood and were happy with what they already had. Who wanted to look like a damn donkey? Well, some people did, but Miss Kim wasn't into making people look like donkeys. I was into realistic enhancements. The customers who were determined to get it super-sized against my judgment often sought out someone else to do the job. Most of the time, it turned out to be a disaster.

There is a young lady right now who has written a book detailing her journey with butt shots. Baaay-bee, she looks absolutely horrible. I still have a hard time believing that someone actually did that to her body. She kept getting shots and wouldn't stop, even after her butt was huge. I read that she started getting really lumpy. Someone told her the only way to get rid of the lumps was to get more injections.

I do know that injecting the silicone into and around the lumps can *sometimes* break up the silicone. It can smooth out the clumps. But that is a temporary fixture and not the proper procedure for repairing that type of problem.

Ladies who did see my work and were pleased with the results sought me out. Not just to do a butt job, but sometimes to repair a butt job that went all bad. Some of these girls were too far gone and there was nothing I could do. The ones I could help, I did. I also didn't always feel comfortable going behind someone else's work either. Imagine getting a painting done by one person, and another person coming behind them and adding things. Sometimes it blended, sometimes it didn't.

Some of the clients I turned away would go to someone else who went over my work and occasionally it would destroy their butts. Then, those same females that didn't listen to me in the first place, came back crying, "Please fix me, Miss Kim. Please!" But there was little if anything I could do. All they had to do was listen to me the first time. I felt so sorry for them.

Some of the girls had very bad skin discoloration. Others had horrible lumps. Some had both. I've even seen girls have two butt cheeks that were totally out of symmetry. One was much bigger than the other. Greed will get you nowhere. I didn't wish bad on anyone, but as my grandmother would say, "A hard head can make a soft behind." In these women's cases, a hard head made a hard behind.

Chapter 16

Deaf Ears and Consequences

Even though what I was doing was illegal, I tried to be as cautious as possible. It wasn't my intention to harm anyone, so I had to figure out the safest way to inject the silicone without harmful effects. So I had a minimum amount and a maximum amount I would inject. The minimum was 360 cc's and the most was 720 cc's, which was plenty. Some of my clients would get the maximum amount each time they came, and then act like that still wasn't enough. They were a little too thirsty.

One young lady came to me after going to someone else to get her injections. Her name was Baby Phat and she danced in a strip club in Detroit. Every time she came to see me, she wanted the maximum amount. When I first started on her, she was only a size two at the most. The minimum and maximum amounts differed in not just the quantity of the silicone, but in pricing as well.

She kept coming back. I told her I wouldn't inject her anymore. Many clients weren't trying to take no for an answer. They wanted more. They said things like, "Forty will give you as many shots as you want for a thousand dollars. With her you don't have to wait and keep coming back."

After explaining the dangers of over injecting, I told them, "Okay. Well, go to Forty then." They could go wherever they wanted and spend their money with whomever they pleased. It was their bodies and their money. I did all I could do to warn them.

My main concern was safety. Injecting too much at once could be harmful. Even life-threatening. I told them each and every time, but it fell on many deaf ears.

Well, Baby Phat went to Forty and got more injections. She let Forty give her unsafe amounts of whatever it was she was pumping her syringes with. This was definitely a big mistake, especially since Baby Phat had already had so much work done already.

It wasn't until about three months later that I saw Baby Phat again. Baaaay-beeee! Let me tell you, honey, that young lady was messed up something terrible. Her butt was lumpy all over. There was no smoothness at all. One side drooped much lower than the other, and her butt was now crooked and had a lot of discoloration. The poor chile was in despair.

I tried to hide my facial expression from her. I don't know if I was successful or not, but it was hard to miss someone's mouth hanging down to the floor. I was shocked. I just couldn't believe somebody would do that to someone else. This Forty chick needed to be off the streets.

That wasn't the end of Baby Phat's problems. You see, Forty had injected her solution near the folds of her butt crack. That is a definite NO-NO! That area is near main arteries. It is dangerous to inject there if you do not know what you are doing. Like I mentioned earlier, it could send the solution straight to the heart or lungs.

There were so many lumps, it looked as though she had large cysts all over her behind. I wanted to cry for her. She had disfigured herself all because of unresolved deep insecurities. Her perception of herself was clouded and warped. I held back the tears I wanted to shed. Really, I wanted to cry because there was nothing I could do to help. Her life would be affected in more ways than one. She was a dancer, and that is how she fed her children. That career was definitely over. Her botched butt injections were beyond basic repair. The only thing she could possibly do was see a plastic surgeon. She needed reconstructive work.

Because most surgeons shied away from such a risky operation to avoid any further disfigurement, her options were limited. She begged me to help. It was so sad, but Miss Kim couldn't do anything. I wouldn't dare mess with that.

Baby Phat wasn't the only one, or the first case I'd seen like that. I encountered that type of horrendous situation several times. I've had my share of experiences. Many girls seeking out the shots did not want to go through the process slowly. They wanted instant gratification, but in life that is not always possible. Not without consequences.

Girls like this had deeper problems than any needle, syringe, or silicone could ever fix. They had damaged self-image and low self-esteem. I understand the stripper lifestyle is highly competitive, but you have to draw the line somewhere. There is always going to be a girl with firmer thighs, toner arms, a bigger butt or larger breasts. Variety is what makes the world go-round. At some point, you have to know when enough is enough.

I don't think some of them would have ever stopped until some circumstance would have forced them to. The never-ending desire to want more was like going into a cell that you could never get out of. It imprisoned your happiness and held you captive in a sea of dissatisfaction. Rather than using their minds to find happiness, that which is limitless, they looked to the body, which is extremely limited.

Any choice to do anything to your body, including any type of alteration, should be guided by some level of common sense. We're all imperfect, and there is nothing wrong with making changes to yourself. There is, however, something wrong when you don't know how to flick the off button, or when you ignore the warning lights flashing before you.

You can't go from Flatty Patty to a Nicki Minaj physique overnight. Not in one session. This generation wants everything right away. The microwavable version. Don't they know that slow oven roasted is always better?

It is no secret that I'm a fan of doing what you want to fix or enhance yourself physically. I am, however, not an extremist, and I don't support acts of extremism. I realized that I couldn't "fix" everyone who came to me. Some of the flaws they wanted corrected were not physical at all. That's why I always spoke to the women first, so I could inquire about why they really wanted the procedure done. I wanted to make sure they were not doing it for the wrong reasons.

Some girls were so pretty with beautiful shapes naturally. Why risk messing up what God had already given you? Sometimes certain requests just didn't make sense. I learned that no matter what I said, the best teacher was experience. Unfortunately, not all experiences were good.

Chapter 17

Very Noticeable

Seeing celebrities was the norm for me, and I worked on quite a few of them. To me, they were just regular people who happened to be in the spotlight for all the world to see. The only setback regarding me working on celebrities was they never gave me any referrals. I attended celebrity parties, award shows, and other gatherings, but because they were so secretive about the fact they had gotten butt shots, they would act as though they didn't know me. So them giving someone my information was out of the question. They didn't want anybody else to say, "Well, how did you get her info? Did you have any work done?" It was like taboo to them. And because I only gained clients by referrals, I didn't really care about gaining celebrities as clients.

I guess they felt better thinking that everybody in the public and all their fans just simply wouldn't notice. The girl I worked on who was an up and coming rapper and singer had her work done before she was in the public eye. People didn't really know who she was. She was smart, because she did it at the onset of her career. Her new look is all people saw. There are no old pictures to compare her to.

I've had several clients come to me who were already very famous. It was senseless to be so secretive when for the last twenty years the whole world already knew what you looked like. Yes, honey, this celebrity woman was a famous singer. She had been out of commission for a few years struggling with that monkey on her back. But she was trying to make a comeback, and everybody was generally hoping she would conquer her problems. She definitely had her share of drama, but still, she had a one of a kind voice. The whole world knew her. When she called me to come and see her, the first thing I wanted to do was feed her. She was so skinny.

I explained that we could do small amounts of injections to give her a little more roundness, but nothing too drastic because it wouldn't match her thin body. Her main concern was secrecy, and that I could understand. You could have put a raisin in her butt and it would have been noticeable. That's how skinny she was. She just kept telling me she didn't want anybody to know and I couldn't tell anyone. I didn't plan on telling anyone, and I tried my best to explain it wouldn't benefit me to tell anyone. She was outright paranoid about anyone finding out.

I was looking at her like: people have had posters of you ever since the late eighties. They have you plastered on their bedroom walls and have followed your every move. How she thought people wouldn't notice her walking around suddenly with a big butt, was a mystery to me. She was so worried about people talking about it. I was surprised because people were already talking about her already very public issues. She came to me with a non-disclosure agreement she wanted me to sign, promising never to say anything about the work she wanted done to her butt.

Honey, please! I had to respectfully decline. The rumor was that she and her husband were heavily into drugs, and she definitely looked the part. So I asked her without trying to outright offend her, "If you were on drugs and had to deal with a drug dealer, do you think that person would tell your business? No, because telling your business would be the same as them telling on themselves."

I didn't want to seem harsh, but she said, "Oh, okay gotcha!" Why in the world would I put my name on anything and what I was doing was illegal? I don't think so.

She was beautiful and fine just how she was, and she didn't need a big butt to make a comeback. Her priority should have been on strengthening her vocal chords. I wish she'd had the chance to have accomplished that. She left this earth before her time.

By then I had been going to New York doing injections for about three years. I had a client by the name of Christy who worked in a strip club. She was very petite and had a really nice body already. She only wanted me to fill in a few dents she had. Nothing over-the-top.

Christy had a referral for me, and she came to see me with her mom, sister, and the lady whom she'd referred. The woman who wanted the injection was one of Christy's mom's customers. They were all Italian, and Christy felt it proper to explain they were part of a Mafia family. I guess she wanted to let me know ahead of time in case it would sway me from doing any future business with her.

Chile, please! I worked with clients from all walks of life. What people did was their own business, and I couldn't care less. As long as my life wasn't in any danger, it didn't matter.

The day they came to see me, I wasn't feeling well. I almost cancelled because I didn't feel up to it, but I went on ahead anyway. I promised Christy I'd meet with them, and I didn't like to disappoint clients.

When I finally met them, I was happy I did. They are some extremely nice people. We spent a good amount of time talking, laughing, and just getting to know each other. I met some more of their family and close friends.

One of the older women with them wanted to get her butt done also. She was about sixty-five years old.

"Sweetie, why do you wanna do your butt now?" I asked, thinking she was the oldest client I'd ever had.

"Girl, I still need to look sexy. My husband is in prison in upstate New York. He's allowed conjugal visits," she said proudly.

"So you mean, y'all get to do it?"

"We sure do. And he loves to slap my ass!" she said, winking.

"I know that's right." We cracked up laughing, and I agreed to do the procedure on her. After she got her injections, they asked if I would come with them to meet the rest of the family. They lived out in Staten Island, New York. I learned that many Mafia-tied families lived out in Staten Island.

One of the sisters I met was a very tall lady. As a matter of fact, you know I've dealt with a lot of drag queens in my day, and I can usually spot one pretty easily. However, I must say, with this lady, I wasn't sure. She had a very deep and raspy voice like she smoked ten packs of cigarettes a day. But yes, she definitely was all woman, honey, and was such a cool and down-to-earth person.

We all hung out while I was in New York. They picked me up and took me to the youngest sister's house. She also lived in Staten Island. When we pulled up to the house, I was like "WOW!" I couldn't believe it. The house was huge. It damn near took up the entire block. It was immaculate too. Something out of the magazines.

The youngest sister had a six-year-old daughter and this little girl was already a fashionista. She rocked a pair of $200 jeans, and her little fingernails were professionally manicured. She had tips on them and everything. She was too cute and she knew it. We all had a blast hanging out. We kicked it for a long while, relaxing and having a few drinks.

The Backside of the Story

The oldest sister (the big one), told me that she was opening a bar and wanted me to come to the grand opening. Unfortunately, I was unable to attend. But honey, the next time I saw them, they were all on television. Their show became very popular and had top ratings. It was a reality show about people tied to the mob.

One of the sisters even ended up with her own spin-off show. She definitely deserved it because that lady is full of life and is too funny. She kept me laughing and very entertained during the time we spent together. Now, I just crack up laughing whenever I turn on the TV and see her on her show acting up. All of those ladies are some of the coolest women I have ever met. Especially the big one. And for the record . . . no, I did not do her lips.

Another client whom I am very fond of, taped a season of the *Bad Girls Club* and was on the second season of *Basketball Wives of L.A.*. I met her through a mutual friend in Atlanta. She was in town at that time for the Fourth of July weekend. My friend called and asked if I was in town, because someone wanted to make an appointment to see me that evening. I had plans and was going to say I couldn't because it was the holiday. But she begged me because her friend was flying back to L.A. the next day. I agreed to meet up with them and that's how I was introduced to the young lady from *Basketball Wives*.

She and her friends were so much fun. When we met up, they were chilling with these ballers, honey, and these dudes were splurging like crazy on them. We ended up at the Inter-Continental Hotel in Buckhead, Atlanta. They had a really nice suite with several rooms and those dudes were in one of them.

"So are you ready to do the shots?" I asked.

"Yeah, girl, do you have all of your supplies?" she asked.

"I do, but don't you want to get those dudes out of here? You don't want to get injections with them right there in the next room do you?"

"Girl, please. We don't care what they think. We ready to get this shit done!" I couldn't believe it. They were laughing and carefree.

"Well, okay then," I said. "If y'all don't care, then I'm good too!"

"Where do you want us to lay?" they asked.

I laugh every time I think about it. Any other time, I would have been trippin' about having men in the same suite, but these guys were cool and laid back. I felt comfortable and at ease with them. Besides, we had some privacy. They were staying in a topnotch hotel and the suite had separate rooms. That's how these girls did things.

They were prepared too. Honey, they came with magazines and pictures of butts, so I could have a good idea of what look she was going for. She already had a very nice shape. She was modeling for *Fed*, *Diva*, *Smooth* and *Honey* already. She felt she could get more work if she did some butt enhancements. It worked, because she was all over the place afterward.

She's already a beautiful girl. Her dark chocolate skin was almost flawless. She has penetrating, big brown eyes. And that hair! Honey, she has beautiful, thick, long hair down her back. At first, I thought it was a really good weave. Maybe fusion. But I can tell you with 100% certainty that it is authentic.

The young lady had the sweetest disposition, and I just loved her voice. I must say, she is a very pleasant girl. One thing I admire about her is her drive and focus. That girl has a serious work ethic. She knew the type of industry she was in, and she knew what she needed to look like in order to be at the top of her game.

I can remember the first time I gave her and her friends the injections. They were so geeked about it. Before I even finished her, she was asking how soon before she could come back and get it done again. Most of the time, after all that pain, people weren't thinking about the next session. But she was ready, baby. I think with every poke she saw dollar signs, and she explained to me why she was so adamant about it.

"I have a bigger plan, and I know what's necessary for me to get this money."

A couple of years later, she was offered a spot on *Basketball Wives of L.A.* She was going to use the show as a platform to open bigger doors. This girl was definitely a hard worker and stayed focused. Everything was on point with her, down to her exercise and diet regiment. She was an anomaly, because most celebrities didn't stay in contact with me, or let anyone know they even knew me. But not her. She was and still is in contact with me, being a great friend supporting me. She even continued to do so during my time away in prison. I will always appreciate her for that.

Chapter 18
What Was I Thinking?

By the year 2007, my business was really in full effect. I was doing extremely well. I had over 500 clients that I serviced, but I had done at least 1,500 injections since many of them were repeats. I think the first revelation of what I was doing happened when I enrolled my oldest son in college. To be able to pay for his tuition out of pocket was an honor.

We were sitting in the auditorium during his orientation, and he had to fill out some information. I remember it like it happened yesterday. The form asked for my occupation. He asked, "What do you want me to put on this form? Do you build houses, or are you a doctor or a nurse?" I knew he was being sarcastic, but it really stuck with me. *Oh my God! What am I?*

My name was starting to appear all over the Internet. I was talked about in hair salons, strip clubs, and on blogs. I wasn't excited about being all over the Internet, because I was trying to be careful since the business was illegal. So many people had heard about "Miss Kim," honey.

With all that going on, it was hard for me to find a moment of peace. I needed some spiritual stability to keep me sane in the wild black market business I was in. Initially, I vowed never to do business in Atlanta since that's where I lay my head and where my church home was.

For about ten years I had been actively involved in my church. It was a trip, honey, because no one at the church knew what I was doing.

I'd go out of town to meet up with clients, do some work, and come back with plenty of money and live a normal life. At least what I considered a normal life. I had to keep that frame of mind. Your mindset shapes your reality. The way we interpret our actions is what allows us to continue doing whatever it is we're doing, whether it's right or wrong.

As long as I was at home enjoying my family, going to church praising God, and paying my tithes, I was able to categorize myself as a normal person. I stayed active in several of the church's auxiliaries. I kept a smile on my face, but in private hours when I was all alone, I prayed to God about this secret life I was living.

Honestly, I was confused. I felt like, regardless of the fact that what I was doing was illegal, I was still helping people reshape their lives and contributing to them feeling good about themselves. That's what I told myself in order to carry on and justify my actions. This business wasn't easy for me. Not emotionally. I had my reservations, but no matter how many times I thought about quitting, that one person in need always pulled me back in.

Justification leads to continuation.

Continuation leads to complacency.

Complacency leads to being comfortable ...

Then, once I grew comfortable, that's when danger invited itself. It saw a weak spot where it could creep in and wreak havoc. All because I'd found a reason to justify the law-breaking action I was doing. Every now and then there would be a moment when I couldn't hide behind my own rationale. When the fear of being exposed took over my entire body.

For example, I was at Hartsfield, the Atlanta International Airport. While waiting at baggage claim, I was on the phone

105

talking to my church's co-pastor. I was on my way home after doing injections in Detroit.

My pastor was very fond of me and held me in high regards. While we were speaking, this girl came up to me.

"Excuse me! Excuse me! Ain't you Miss Kim?" she asked. I was on the phone, so I didn't really acknowledge her. But that didn't deter her at all.

"Miss Kim, right! You don't remember me?"

"No!" I mouthed. I couldn't tell the co-pastor of my church to hold on, without being rude, because she was in the middle of explaining something.

"How you don't remember me, Miss Kim? You did my ass! Don't you remember?" she said as she turned to show it to me.

Lawd, I was so embarrassed. This girl wasn't exactly quiet either. I paused for a moment because I just knew she exposed me. I was sure my co-pastor heard and was going to say something. When she didn't, I exhaled and shooed the girl away. Thank goodness she was too busy talking. That would have been a hard one to get out of. I wouldn't have known what to do. I sang on the Praise Team. I was a youth leader and worked very closely with the co-pastor. She would have been very disappointed in me.

Moments like the airport incident were the times I came closest to really wanting to quit. *Kim, what are you doing? Why are you risking everything? You know you are breaking the law. You could go to jail. You could be taken away from your children. It's not worth it.*

Yes, I would try to talk some sense into my own crazy self.

Another time, the complete opposite happened. I was in the mall in the dressing room trying on some clothes, and I stepped out to look in the larger mirror. A young lady stepped out beside me and was twisting and turning, asking her friend if she liked her dress. I recognized the girl. I did her butt. She looked up and saw me too.

"Oh my God! . . . Miss Kim!" she said. Before I could get a word out, she was hugging me. Then I realized she was crying. "I've wanted to call you so many times, but I lost your number."

"You all right?" I asked.

"All right? Miss Kim, I am one *thousand* times better than all right. My life has been so much better ever since you did my butt. I just feel so confident and sexy. I love my new look. I love it, love it, love it! Thank you so much."

This girl was on cloud nine. She was really happy, smiling and blushing. I felt good inside knowing I played a part in making this girl feel confident. Moments like that regenerated my irrational thinking. This part of me would say, *Kim, girl, you aren't hurting anyone. You are doing a good thing. So what you aren't medically qualified. You're providing a great service. It's all right. Everybody should have the opportunity to have what they want and something to make them feel good about themselves. We only get one life. Hey, it worked out for you.*

That is what I would tell myself, and it would be the stronger voice than the one telling me to stop. I listened to the stronger voice. I lost my grip on reality.

Chapter 19

Exceptions to the Rule

Business was so crazy that in order to get a little peace, I would have to cut my phone off. Some of my clients were ruthless. I half expected some of them to show up in the supermarket when I was shopping for groceries. The ones who had gotten it done already, were by far the most aggressive. They got their first taste of something good and would do anything to get more.

Once they achieved a certain look, I wouldn't inject anymore. Period. I had to block some of their numbers so they couldn't call me. Some of them were way too 'thirsty,' as I liked to call it. Sometimes that didn't even work, because they would call me from a number that I didn't recognize, and I'd answer not knowing it was one of the "thirsties."

They would say, "Hello . . . Miss Kim? Please, please don't hang up. This is—"

"I told you, no more injections. I told you the last time, that was it for you."

"But, I'll pay you double!"

"No!"

"Please, Miss Kim, just a little bit more. I'll pay you double and add a nice tip, please."

"No. You already have enough. Anything else will be overdoing it. It will be too much."

"I just want a little filled in one spot, please."

Honey, the conversation would go on and on. They were a trip. I usually stuck to my word, and on very few occasions, I'd give in. Sometimes, they would show up with a friend or two that they referred. Some referrals I knew about, some I didn't. They would act as if they were just coming along to be supportive. The next thing I knew, they would get on the table. That used to really irritate me because I very concerned about the end result. But hey, that was the nature of the business.

Once in New York, I met a couple of Dominican ladies. Someone referred them to me. They were sisters and were very attractive with the bodies to go with it. They had a very exotic look. When I tell you these ladies had their bodies together, trust and believe they really did. They wanted to have their hips done.

Their waist couldn't have been more than a size 24 or 25. Their breasts were about a size 38D, and their butts were already plump. They explained they'd previously had some work done. They showed me their breasts, which were implants, and it was some of the best work I had ever seen. Trust me, over the years I had seen my share of cosmetic surgeries, so I definitely knew when somebody had good work.

Their breast implants were called "gummy bears." It was a type of silicone implant that felt real to the touch. The breasts had a natural drop to them. They weren't hoisted up to their shoulders like some that I'd witnessed, and you would never know they had implants. It was also difficult to tell because they were placed behind the muscle, which I learned is the best way to have implants.

Both ladies also didn't like the size of their areolas, so they had those done as well. Now they were about the size of quarters and looked absolutely perfect. Whoever their doctor was, he or she had done an excellent job.

One sister had an abdominoplasty, and the incision line was barely visible. Oh yes, this doctor did tight work. I had to know who he or she was. We started talking about all kinds of procedures they either had done or knew someone that had it done. These girls were the nip and tuck queens.

By the time they finished talking, I couldn't contain my excitement. I asked them where they had their procedures done. I really wasn't too sure if they would tell me, but surprisingly, they didn't hesitate. Some of my clients could be so secretive. They said, "The Dominican Republic, mami." I was surprised, but after seeing other people who also had some work done in the DR, I realized the cosmetic surgeons there were very talented and thorough.

There, the surgeons didn't put you to sleep because it was too dangerous, but they induced a twilight sleep. You weren't completely unconscious; you were just incoherent. Which was definitely a plus, considering some of the complications involved with general anesthesia. After talking to them, I now understood why on most of the Spanish channels, many of the women looked so good. Access to a good surgeon was simple and affordable.

I know typically they say, "You get what you pay for," but there are a few exceptions to that rule. In the Dominican Republic (DR) I learned that you can have some procedures done at only a fraction of the cost you would pay here in the United States.

When I found out that my Dominican *Mamis* were planning a trip back to the DR, I asked them to let me know when, so I could join them. This could be a wonderful opportunity for both my clients and me.

Quite a few of my clients wanted other work done, like lipo, tummy tucks, or breast jobs, but couldn't get it done without breaking their pockets because of how expensive it is here in the states.

Sometimes, I would have to turn some clients away because they needed to lose weight. Some would come and their stomachs would be bigger than their butts would ever be. I knew they would be dissatisfied with the injections if they couldn't even see it because of excessive body fat. Some would lose the weight and then complain about too much excessive skin. They would research plastic surgeons for a body lift. The price sometimes would be in the excess of $20,000 or more. My clients would be so discouraged because they couldn't afford it. And because most insurance companies don't cover cosmetic surgeries, they would be stuck.

One exception the insurance companies made was for breast reductions. But even then that surgery is done for medical reasons. The insurance company will cover it if the patient is having back problems because of their breasts being so heavy. But even that required so much red tape. I felt good knowing that I might possibly have a solution for them.

I didn't want to sell anyone a dream and take their hard earned money, unless I could really help them and give them the results they were looking for. This trip might help change a lot of things. Trust me, giving someone a bigger butt who already had a stomach hanging down to their mid-thigh would not be right. What kind of hot mess would that be? I couldn't put my name on something like that. I'd never get a referral again. Chile, please!

About two months later, I made the trip to the Dominican Republic with my clients. I dragged one of my good friends along because I didn't want to go alone.

OMG! I loved it. Actually saying I loved it is an understatement. We stayed in the capital, Santo Domingo, home to many professional baseball players that play in the US.

The DR has wonderful beaches, wonderful people, and best of all, wonderful cosmetic surgeons. My Spanish wasn't good, so my newfound Dominican friends took me around to different doctors and translated for me.

Their offices were nice and updated. Professionalism was very important, and I felt comfortable talking openly to these doctors. They showed me before and after pictures, and some of these people had been literally transformed. Making beautiful bodies was an art, not just a job to these doctors. They knew their craft.

I discussed the possibility of getting some of my clients to come to the DR, and how I could help them grow their business with American clientele. They were happily in agreement.

Overall, I had a great time in the DR. By the time I left, I made several connections and networked my way to many surgeons and even a few cosmetic dentists. I had several clients who were interested in getting their mouth together. Veneers and Lumineers are very expensive in the States. The average price per tooth can be as expensive as $2,000! Doing your entire mouth can easily run you $40,000! I know firsthand.

In the DR, you could have your entire mouth done for nowhere near those prices. I felt a sense of comfort knowing I would be able to refer my clients to these dentists as well. I had clients that desired implants and complete oral reconstruction. It had only been a dream for many of them. Now it could be a reality.

As a result of meeting up with this new network of doctors, I was able to work out some really good deals. The doctors were willing to take their already inexpensive prices and reduce them even further based on the number of patients that I brought at one time, depending on the type of procedure they had done. The whole thing just kept getting better and better and kind of just fell into place.

I tried to think of everything ahead of time to make the whole experience as simple and as comfortable as possible for both my clients and doctors. I was definitely going to make this opportunity beneficial for everyone involved.

Chapter 20

International Clients

I was pleasantly surprised to find out that many doctors in the US gave doctors in the DR their props. Dominican cosmetic surgeons have a very good reputation in the international medical community. That in itself furthered my excitement.

Before I took anyone back to the DR, I needed to resolve a few things. I made sure I did my due diligence. I read everything I could find on the Internet about the doctors I met. Sometimes it was difficult to find out a lot about them, but I researched as much as I could. Some surgeries had very quick recovery times. Others were more intense. However, every surgery required some level of aftercare and follow up. I was already aware of some doctors not wanting to remove silicone or go behind another surgeon's work. I truly believed it would be challenging to find doctors in the US who would provide aftercare for clients coming from the DR.

Most of my clients had jobs, families, and obligations that limited the amount of time they could spend in another country. They would need to see a local cosmetic surgeon shortly after they returned. I made sure they had passports and whatever other documents they needed. Some of them had never been out of the country; some had never even been on a plane before!

I told my clients to make sure they went to see their primary care provider and a cosmetic surgeon before making plans to travel. Also, I gave them a list of questions to ask. I even told them the necessary blood work they needed, and I recommended they have it done before going. I couldn't have them wasting their money and their tests weren't normal.

In addition to the blood work, I needed them to make sure they would have an aftercare provider. After networking with some of my clients in various states, I found doctors who were willing to provide aftercare. I was prepared to possibly have to search for months. But I was shocked when only a few doctors declined.

Many states had doctors who were willing to do this, and it felt like everything was going to work out.

With the surgeons in the DR ready to receive my referrals, and with the aftercare in the States taken care of, there was only one thing left to do, honey: take my clients to get the services they desired.

It wasn't long before four of my clients wanted to make the trip to the Dominican Republic. They were geeked and excited about it. I don't know if they were more amped or if I was. I always felt good about being able to help people. I had everything planned.

Two of them wanted tummy tucks. They'd wanted tummy tucks for a long time, but couldn't afford it. Not in America. The procedure would only cost them $2,900 instead of the average $7,000 that it costs in the US.

We arrived a few days early so I could give them a chance to sightsee and have a little fun. Plus, it gave me a chance to make sure everything was in place. I made all the necessary arrangements ahead of time because I wanted to display professionalism.

One of the doctors arranged for a driver to pick us up from the airport. He spoke fluent English and was very nice. We spent the first day getting settled. I took them to meet their doctor, do their

115

blood work again, and complete all the prerequisites before the procedure. These doctors were very thorough. I wanted to make sure my clients were completely comfortable with the doctors doing their procedures. It was important. We went to the beach and had fun sightseeing. There is nothing like having a little fun. I was happy I could do this for my clients. They got double the fun. A wonderful trip and a new body at the end. It just didn't get any better.

Everything went better than I planned for a first trip. It went so well that it eventually became a regular routine for me. I started to make those trips every four to six months with my clients that wanted procedures done. The average time they would stay after having the surgery was about five days. Sometimes, their stay would be longer or shorter depending on how much time was needed for recuperation.

Some clients opted to stay in the hospital after the procedure. Even though most of the procedures were outpatient surgeries, they stayed because it was convenient. You could remain in the hospital for an average of about $50 a day. Definitely unheard of in the US. The doctors also put together an aftercare house they could go to if they didn't want to stay in the hospital. They'd have a private nurse look after them. I even had a few clients choose to stay in a hotel and pay a nurse to stay with them.

The only thing my clients did for me was pay my travel expenses. And honey, I didn't travel any way other than first class. The true payment was once the procedures were done and the expression on their faces when they looked in the mirror. That made it all worth it and was truly priceless.

My clients didn't mind footing my bill since I was saving them thousands of dollars. They were more than happy to take care of my expenses.

There is something I must say in regards to surgeons in the Dominican Republic: they are definitely on point. Don't for one minute think that because it's a so-called third world country their medical practices aren't up to par. Baby, most of their doctors go to Europe or the United States for training, so they know what they are doing. Honestly, I have seen better work over there in many cases than I've seen over here.

The Dominican Republic is a Spanish-speaking Caribbean country. The doctors there know how to contour a body and perfect the curvature of a woman. Especially a woman of color, because they are the primary population, and Dominican men love curvaceous women.

The majority of my clients who traveled to the DR were from New York. It's a diverse place, and people from many countries you probably never knew existed lived in New York, honey. I loved it!

Another one of my clients that I started building a strong working relationship with was a lady named Madeline. She was Puerto Rican and danced at the popular strip club the *Hustler* in New York. She had beautiful teeth. Her smile looked perfect.

I had visited several cosmetic dentists in Atlanta, and I was trying to decide if I was going to get veneers. I think a smile is so important. There is nothing like a set of pretty, pearly white teeth.

The cheapest price I could find was $20,000 for what I wanted done. I was trying to decide if I was going to get it done in Atlanta or the DR. I decided to ask Madeline about hers.

"Where did you have your teeth done?" I asked. "They look so good, girl."

"I didn't have them done here!" she boasted.

"Well, what state did you go to?" I asked.

"No, girl. I didn't have it done in the United States. It was too expensive."

"Where did you go?"

"Costa Rica," she replied.

"Whaaaat! For real, girl? How much was it? Because the cheapest price I got was twenty grand." She shocked me with her answer.

"About $5,000." I couldn't believe it. That short conversation had me online researching the dentist that did her work. That was a very reasonable price. Since I had been thinking of having my teeth done anyway, I decided it wouldn't hurt to check out Costa Rica. And once I found out they had a rainforest, it became much more enticing.

You already know what I did next. That's right! I hopped my butt on the next thing smoking and went to Costa Rica, San Jose to be exact. I set up a consultation with the dentist to get an examination and an estimate.

Their office was state of the art, honey, and once again, I felt comfortable in another country. She was on the money about their pricing because they quoted me $8,000. That sounded so much better than $20,000.

I stayed in Costa Rica for an additional four days vacationing. I toured the island and of course, went to the rainforest. I made my appointment to have my dental work two months later.

Getting veneers is a process. When I first went back, I stayed for five days getting my prep work done. They took molds and impressions initially, so that everything was a perfect fit for my mouth. I returned home with temporaries, and I scheduled an appointment for three weeks later to get my permanent veneers and crowns.

The Backside of the Story

When I came back to the States, my regular dentist was impressed with the work I had done. He said it was of quality. In my opinion and from my experience, the DR is ranked #1 on my list for their cosmetic surgeries. Also ranked #1 on my list is Costa Rica for their dentistry. Of course, that's just my personal opinion, but it's backed by the countless good work that I've personally witnessed. And the eyes don't lie, honey.

Chapter 21

Obsession

A book titled *African Queen: The Real Life of the Hottentot Venus* written by Rachel Holmes, depicts the life of an African woman by the name of Saartjie Baartman, (pronounced Sarkey). She was only twenty-one when she was taken from the Eastern Cape of South Africa and shipped to London to be a "specimen" of beauty and an exhibition for Europeans who were obsessed with her butt. (Not much different than the girls we see in videos and on television with their backside being the center of attraction.)

Back in the 1800s when Baartman was captured, she was mysterious. The likes of such voluptuousness had never been seen before until the African continent had been pillaged. In Europe, this African Queen was ridiculed, yet worshipped.

Baartman was born an orphan in South Africa, and no one was around to protect her. Her father was murdered, and the only other men in her life were those who wanted her strictly for sexual entertainment. Her 200-year-old story sounds like countless other modern stories about Black women, who come from fatherless homes. The only men in their lives, being the ones who want to exercise some form of sexual control over them, or see them as pure entertainment.

Deep beneath the surface of a booty-poppin', ass-shaking woman, was some memory of the pain attached to being seen as a sex object for hundreds of years. Resistance was once unheard of, and submission and acceptance of a woman's role in society had been mandatory if she wanted to survive. We are not far removed from that time and place in history.

If we could get brain injections that made us smarter as opposed to butt injections, the scary thing is that the line for butt injections would probably run ringlets around the line for brain injections.

We are so obsessed with our physical appearance that our mental health and self-esteem get neglected. You see, the mind is internal, and without some form of expression, nobody would know how great someone's mind is, as opposed to having that ideal shape, where there's instant gratification from onlookers.

I can tell you for certain, there is no substitute for a deep self-love and strong mindedness that comes from within. No matter the shape of your behind, if your mind is weak, then you are what you think. People will use you and throw you away if that's all you have.

When I went out clubbing with my friends before I got my injections, I didn't fully enjoy myself. I was too worried about how I looked and how other people thought I looked. I had self-esteem issues. Because I didn't have a big, juicy booty didn't make me any less beautiful, unless I thought I was less beautiful. It was a burden I applied to myself unnecessarily because of what I thought others thought of me.

How can one body part be more valuable than the whole being? When we look at it that way, we see the ridiculousness associated with obsessing about it. The obsession leads to desperate risk-taking, such as going into a hotel room and getting a black market procedure to look a certain way.

Don't get me wrong, I don't think there is anything wrong with changing something about yourself. The problem is when that change is so important to you, that without it, you feel like you can't enjoy life. A bold act shouldn't come from a place of desperation. It should generate from pride and boldness in a way where you can truly say, "I am happy with or without this alteration. If I choose to do it, it's because it will add to my happiness, not be the creator of it." In that sense, it's all right.

Not everyone shares the same values. Some people don't think you should ever make changes to yourself. I had a friend when I was younger, whose father didn't allow her to shave her legs, relax her hair, or wear any weave. He said she should be happy with the way God made her. Now that she is grown, she has some of the most beautiful natural hair. In her household, her father's words shaped how she thought she should look. In some ways making those small changes would have seemed disrespectful to her father.

As a grown woman, I often heard her speak of possibly relaxing her hair, but she always backs off once she makes her final decision. My point is, even though she's au naturel, she's still not being who she wants to be. Someone else's opinion (her father's), is still shaping who she wants to be today.

Whether you are natural or have had changes done to yourself, the ideal way to be is however *you* choose. Nobody else should be making that choice for you. Just because she hasn't made any alterations doesn't mean she's happy. It's all about developing your own sense of self.

Everyone has their own opinion, or at least they should have. In reality, other people's opinions about you really don't matter and they *shouldn't* matter either. There are so many things in life that we cannot control, so when there is something, such as our own happiness, control that, create it, and maintain it, honey!

See yourself as a unique work of art. No two people are the same. Focus on all the good things about yourself that you like. There is always something you have that another person doesn't.

The Backside of the Story

If you don't like the shape of your breasts, start liking them, because there are some women without breasts at all. If you don't like your butt, just remember there are blind people that don't even know what their butt looks like. Love the skin you're in. You can make changes if that's what you choose to do, just make sure they are for the right reasons. It has taken me more than half of my life to learn to love myself.

Chapter 22

My Greatest Lifeline

In 2008 my business was growing and growing fast. I had so many clients it was insane. As time went on, I met this woman by the name of Taylor. She seemed to be a pretty nice young lady. The woman who referred Taylor had come to see me a few times.

Several months prior, I had done her butt. But something was happening with her rear end that I had never experienced before. Every time she got her injections, her butt just got wider. It only protruded a little. She didn't complain about it, she just said, "We'll try it one more time and see what happens."

I wasn't really expecting her to refer anyone since she wasn't getting the look she desired, but she still referred Taylor. The first time I met Taylor, we clicked immediately and became fast friends.

Taylor kept me laughing. That lady was as funny as ever. She dated several guys at the same time, and in order to keep track, she named them by which day of the week she'd see them. Taylor had a Mr. Monday, Mr. Tuesday, Mr. Wednesday and so forth. She kept her limit to seven, so everybody got their own name and didn't have to share it with anybody else. She also said it kept her from getting their names mixed up.

I cracked up. We were as cool as ever. I'd say, "Well, what if Mr. Monday wants to see you on Thursday?" She always had a funny answer. Everything was good with us until the day I asked her what she did for a living.

The irony is I happened to be giving her injections when I asked her. She told me she was one of Detroit's finest. That's right,

Taylor was a police officer! I couldn't believe it. I was literally in shock.

She was lying across the table with her butt out, and I had gloves on with a needle and syringe in my hand. You know I really almost lost it, right? I didn't know what to do. I just acted like I barely cared and continued to make small talk. I always talked to my clients to keep their minds off the pain.

"Girl, you never told me that," I said.

"OUCHHH!" she said, reacting to me inserting the needle. Don't think the thought of me plunging that needle in and interrogating her like I had her on Guantanamo Bay didn't cross my mind. It certainly did.

"Yeah, girl." She paused because of the pain. "I'm a police officer."

I was about to leave her on that table with just one cheek done, because honey, I was thrown by that. Actually, I was hoping I misheard her the first time, or maybe she was joking. But she wasn't kidding. She was *dead* serious.

I'd gotten quiet and started looking around the room planning my escape. I knew it was about to go down, and I wasn't about to be a sitting duck. She noticed I had gotten quiet. You could hear a mouse piss on cotton in that room, honey.

"Girl, you okay? Why you get so quiet all of a sudden?" she asked. Why did she think?

I answered her nonchalantly, "Oh nothin'." I swallowed hard, and baby, there was a lump in my throat the size of a quarter. Yeah, nothing but thoughts of going to jail were in my head. If she wasn't lying face down on that table and could see my facial expression, she would have seen paranoia written all over it. I was sweating like a slave.

Silently, I began praying real hard. "Lord, please, if you protect me through this last job, I'll get outta here and this woman won't ever, *ever* see me again. Ever!"

I was slipping for real. I should have asked what she did for a living a long time ago. But I had gotten comfortable once again. You're not *ever* supposed to get comfortable when you're doing something illegal. That's the number one rule in the game. The next is, listen to what your gut is telling you. Your intuition was put in place for a reason. It's an internal compass and alarm system that can sense things before you've figured out anything is even wrong.

Taylor, on the other hand, acted as if it were no big deal that she was the damn po-po. I definitely didn't mess with the police. Little did I know she would be the one to offer me one of my greatest lifelines.

Chapter 23

Slipping Again

I didn't know if the young lady who referred Taylor was satisfied with her results because she never called again. That, however, wasn't unusual. Many women would only come once and I wouldn't hear back from them. I knew I could never get her butt to grow outward. From what I could see, the shots didn't really benefit her. She was left with a wide butt and hips she didn't have before. However, as I said before, I never heard from her again. I found out later she wasn't pleased with her results, but because she didn't let me know and didn't complain, I had no idea that she was dissatisfied.

Months later, I got a call from a lady that wanted my services. There was nothing unusual about that because I always got calls from potential clients. The reason this one stuck out in my mind was because I couldn't identify the person who supposedly referred her. When I asked her again who she was, her name didn't register and she wasn't on my client list. I told her "okay" anyway. There I was slipping again.

She had an accent, like maybe she was Hispanic. I told her I would call once I was in her area, but I didn't give a specific date or time. My preference was to keep everything on the down low and be as discreet as possible. I didn't like people tracking my every move. If something was ever going to happen, I surely wouldn't give them a heads up. I liked to ease in town and then let them know.

Many times I said I was going someplace but then I wouldn't show up. That would be that intuition guiding me, telling me, *Kim, don't you get on that plane.* It was just better when I didn't let anyone know what I was doing.

On top of not wanting to get caught up, I didn't want my phone constantly blowing up either. It was so annoying when the same person called every five minutes. "Are you here yet? Are you there yet?" Oh no, I couldn't be having that.

This Latina young lady started calling me every day asking when I was coming. I told her I would let her know, but that didn't faze her. She was as persistent as ever.

The next time I spoke to her, she said, "I am so sorry to keep bothering you, but can you explain your pricing to me?"

I did. I told her how the pricing went and the amount of cc's for each specific amount.

The woman called again asking where I stayed when I came to the "D." She just had all these questions. Eventually, I told her to get all her questions together and call whoever it was that referred her. If they had the procedure done already, they could give her all the details. Then I told her, "Better yet, have them call me."

In any other business, questioning in that fashion would be normal, but in my case I had to always think about protecting myself. I wasn't feeling the whole phone thing. If a client had questions outside of what the referring party could tell them, they would have to wait to speak to me in person. I'd answer anything they wanted to know face to face.

For two weeks straight, she called me every day. I was getting annoyed, and it didn't seem right. On top of that, something told me to stay alert with this person. I didn't know what it was, but I started being very evasive with her. I can remember answering one of her many calls and having an attitude. She didn't care about my tone; she just kept stressing how soon she wanted to get the procedure done. I honestly just thought the woman was a looney bin. My continuous attitude didn't stop her from dialing my number. I finally said to myself, *Let me go meet this woman and get her out of my hair.*

A few weeks later, I flew into town. I got off the plane, retrieved my luggage, and got into a taxi headed to the hotel. As soon as I turned my phone on, I had about eight messages. That wasn't unusual, but I felt an uneasiness come over me. I started checking my messages and they all were from Taylor, the police officer.

Her message was urgent, and she said I needed to call her right away. My heartbeat immediately sped up. When a client calls me and says it's urgent, I always got nervous. Being that this client happened to be a damn cop, I was really on pins and needles. I was a nervous wreck and contemplated not even calling her back and changing my number altogether. A move like that would be detrimental to my business, but prison was worse. I wasn't sure if I was being totally irrational or not. I called her back.

Taylor answered right away, "Hello?"

"Hey, it's me. Kim. What's the emergency?" I asked as calmly as I could, even though I was shaking in my boots.

"Remember the girl that referred me to you?"

"Yes, what about her? I haven't spoken to her in months. What's going on with her?"

"Well, I believe she referred someone to you that you don't need to see."

"Why do you say that?"

"She called me and said that she was trying to set you up with an undercover news reporter, girl."

"Oh my God!"

"Oh my God is right. She was trying to help the reporter come see you."

I was about to say something, but I stayed quiet so I could hear every word Taylor had to say.

"Girl," she continued, "she gave the reporter my number hoping that I would give her an interview since I had the procedure done too."

"I'm so glad you called me," I said.

"It's nothing, Miss Kim. That heifer wanted to come with an undercover camera and recorder," Taylor informed me.

Dang that was a close call.

"So what did she say before y'all ended the call?" I asked.

"She was pleading with me to help get you out to meet her. I asked her for the reporter's phone number so we could set something up."

"You did?"

"Yes. Then I called the reporter and told her that her source didn't know what she was talking about. I never had any procedure like that done, and I didn't want any parts of it."

"Do you still have the reporter's phone number?" I asked.

Taylor still had the number and gave it to me.

I just kept thanking her repeatedly. Honey, I was so grateful.

I called the number and a recording with her voice came on saying, "You have reached Investigative Reporter Julie Martinez with WDIV News. Please leave a message."

Taylor became my lifeline. Now what were the odds of that? The person who kept me from potentially going to prison was a cop.

Life can be very ironic sometimes.

After that situation, I asked Taylor if she would be interested in doing personal security for me. She happily accepted my offer.

She would come and sit with me from the time I arrived in Detroit and started working, until the last client left. I felt so much more secure with her there. I made sure I paid her well, too. If she had to work her regular job, honey, she would call in just to come and sit with me. She told me I paid her in a day what she made in a week.

We became very good friends over the years. She would come in with her Coach clutch bag. Inside of it she kept that .380, just in case someone got any bright ideas. I learned from the first time, and I'd be damned if that happened again without me being prepared to protect myself.

She told me so many stories about working in the police department. I would be in tears laughing at her crazy self. There was always some craziness going on in Detroit. She said she couldn't let a year go by without having to bust a cap in somebody's ass.

Taylor had me rolling and folded over in laughter when she said the last time she shot somebody, she shot them in the butt. I told her, "Yeah, me too."

We had a good time together.

I knew that if anything went down, she wouldn't mind pulling that trigger and asking questions later.

Chapter 24
It's Not That Serious

My thriving business allowed me to travel all over. Any place where I was in high demand, I was there. I had clients in many states. Butt injections had become very, very popular. So popular that all kinds of people popped up on the scene doing injections. Most of the time they wouldn't last very long. They were using any and everything to inject into people. Deaths because of injections were heard about on the news and in magazines.

These people would claim they were using medical grade silicone, but they weren't. It is very difficult to obtain, trust me I know. I was glad I had many connections in the medical field, in and out of the country.

There are different types of silicone on the market, but only one type of silicone was recommended to me. It's called Silikon 1000. It's the most appropriate substance for soft tissue augmentation. Its high levels of purity and low viscosity allows for it to be easily used with a small needle.

It was not cheap, and you had to have connections with a doctor. The US Attorney on my case was pissed that I wouldn't give up any information on the doctor whom I was buying it from. I guess that was one good thing Marvin did for me. He told the US Attorney I was buying the Silikon 1000 from a doctor. He would be with me sometimes when I would meet with the doctor. He was able to keep that much to himself. I suppose it was because he and the doctor had built a good rapport through me. At least people knew I wasn't injecting them with paint thinner, Fix-a-Flat, or some other crazy chemical. What I was using was also used by medical professionals for different things.

Because I made connections with doctors all over, if one could no longer supply me, I always had a backup. I would never tell on a doctor. The way I saw it, why tell on the person who was trying to make sure I did the right thing by using a safer product. That's not the way the game went. However, at the time, that was my rational thinking.

I didn't want my clients to get those horrendous side effects. I tried to be as safe as possible. That doesn't excuse what I was doing, or make it okay, but for my own conscience, I had to act with some level of responsibility and that was my justification.

According to the medical research community, liquid injectable silicone is very controversial still to this date. There are many people on both sides of the table. Critics argue that the problem with silicone is it's just too unpredictable. They claim it doesn't matter if you have it done by a medical professional or by an underground injector (like I used to be), the chances of the silicone moving (migrating) were the same. It wasn't the person, it was the substance.

Migration (when the silicone moves) just simply can't be predicted. There is no answer as to why two people who get injected in the same location, with the same amount of silicone, have different outcomes. The silicone may stay put in person A, but may migrate in person B. It's a risk the recipient takes.

In Detroit, there was a lady whom I called Forty. She was going around injecting people with silicone, I guess. These women were getting messed up badly by this chick.

I remember when she came to me to have the procedure done. She was fresh out of prison and was back doing the same things she got arrested for in the first place. I felt bad for her two small children, and she said she had to do what she knew in order to provide for them. She already had two strikes against her, and one more incident would send her away for a very long time. I didn't want to see that happen. To this day, I don't know why I cared about her and her children's well-being.

She asked if I would teach her how to do injections. It's funny that she happened to ask me at the same time I was considering asking her if she wanted to learn how to do it. My thought at the time was, *This hustle is better than the one she has got going on.* I know you're probably thinking, *How is she going to teach somebody else something, when she isn't even a professional or licensed?* Very true, and I never got a chance to teach her. She just went off on her own.

However, I knew some things because I spent a lot of time talking to doctors and learning about silicone. I asked surgeons as many questions as I could. Every time I met new doctors or traveled out of the country I asked different questions. Especially in the Dominican Republic. Maybe I felt more comfortable talking to them because they were already very familiar with silicone injections.

When I talked to any doctor, I asked things like, "How do I know when I've injected enough? How can I be sure that I'm not injecting into their bloodstream? How long should I make clients wait between sessions? And so on. I asked every question I could think of. The doctors gave me so much information, and it was useful.

They often commended me because I was asking questions. Some would say, "If you're going to do this, you might as well learn and try to keep down the risk of complications to your clients." And because the doctors in the DR had to deal with patients coming to them to have silicone removed because of different complications, they shared a lot with me. I think that's why I didn't have any of those horror stories from my clients.

I'm not glorifying what I was doing. It's not my life anymore. I am simply sharing my story and my personal experiences. I'm happy for the people who say their life is better because of it, but the overall feeling I have now is remorse. It was wrong, and who was I to take on the role of a doctor? That's the role I played, even though I told all of my clients I wasn't a doctor or nurse. What I did was wrong, and I shouldn't have done it because it is illegal. Simple as that.

When Forty came to see me, we talked briefly, and then one other time I planned on taking her under my wing so she could learn. Unfortunately, people aren't always patient. Next thing I know, I'm hearing that Forty is out there doing injections for people. It didn't surprise me, but I was really concerned and felt bad.

My main concern was: what product was she using? I doubted she was getting her hands on medical grade silicone.

People will use anything to inject you. In Britain, a woman lost both her hands, feet, and butt after being injected with bathroom sealant. The same happened to a woman here in the U.S.

When Lonzi did my injections, I trusted him, but I really didn't know what the solution was. My clients trusted me, but there was no way for them to know which cosmetic filler I was really using on them as well.

My clientele was based on referrals, and some of my clients were telling me that their friends who were looking to get injections said they didn't want to come to me. They were going to Forty. They reasoned that Forty would give them as many cc's as they wanted for $1,000. Honey, I could only shake my head.

According to every doctor I spoke to, that was a big no-no. First of all, the gluteus maximus (butt) is just like the stomach. It will only stretch so much at one time. If you keep injecting, the muscle gets to a point that it can't accept anymore. You risk immediate migration. The solution will go somewhere else in your body. That's when you'll start to see those terrible side-effects. Severe scarring, granuloma formations resembling hard rocks or pebbles, discoloration, and a backside that feels like cement. I'm just naming a few of the horrible side effects. The list is long. I can't think of any reason good enough to risk any of that happening just because a person feels like more is better. Chances of injury or harm are greatly increased when you overload your butt. Honey, it's simply just not that serious.

Chapter 25

A First for Me

Referrals were the lifeline of my business. One of my clients referred Marvin, and that's how we met. This was the client that helped me build a business in DC. The woman he was dating at the time wanted to get her butt enhanced. When he called, I asked him how he got my number, and he told me his friend owned *The Penthouse*, a popular strip club in DC. One of the strippers there gave him my information. Of course, she told him, "Miss Kim is the best!" She referred so many clients to me that when I was charged, the Feds assumed she was a part of a ring I had going. I told them definitely not. This lady never asked me for anything. Not one dime. She did it because of my reputation in the business. She knew my work was good.

From the moment I first spoke with Marvin, he started bombarding me with all sorts of questions. I told Marvin to have his girl call me so we could talk about what she wanted.

"Why can't you just talk to me about it?" he boldly asked.

"I only speak to the person who is actually having the procedure done. I never speak to significant others."

"But baby, I'm the one spending the money, and all money spends the same," was his comeback.

"Look, I don't care about your money, because if I don't speak to her, money won't be involved."

"Just tell me what she needs to know, and I'll pass the information along." He just wasn't getting it.

"Either she calls me, or you can lose my number." I figured that was one potential client I may have lost. It kind of bothered me for a moment, because the lady who referred him always referred some good people, and I didn't want to mess it up.

It was just something about his voice that irritated me. He wasn't mean or anything. Marvin was just a smooth talker, and it kind of rubbed me the wrong way. Also, I didn't talk to men because they made me paranoid. I've had some bad past experiences, and I just didn't feel comfortable dealing with them. Not in this business at least.

I called my client that referred him, and I told her how he was talking. She laughed and said, "That sounds like Marvin. He is harmless, girl. He is just a smooth talker."

Minutes later, his girlfriend called me. I said what I had to say, and she asked several questions. I thought we covered all the preliminary details, but once we were done, he still wanted to talk to me. He insisted I explain everything all over.

"I already worked out all the details with your girl. If you want to know anything else, ask her."

"But I can't get the details from her like I can from you," he said.

"Okay," I said, wanting to get him off the line, "I will tell you this. You guys have to fly to Atlanta to see me. I told her to call me once the arrangements are made."

How did I know that it would be him calling me with the arrangements? He was nose deep in the process.

They flew in the next weekend and called me. When I got their hotel information, I went to meet them. I knocked on the door, and of course, Marvin let me in. He had a big smile on his face and just stood in the doorway.

When he wouldn't move I asked, "What are you smiling about?"

He said, "So you're the one with the mouth!" I didn't feed into his games, because I was here strictly on business. Politely, I smiled and proceeded to check my surroundings to make sure I was safe.

Whenever I was home, I didn't have any security because I didn't normally have clients in Atlanta, unless someone flew in to see me. So I had to be very careful. I wasn't feeling the situation with a man in the room.

However, I can say this: I did compliment him in my mind. I thought he was nice looking, but a little shorter than I imagined. His swag was kind of on point though. Yeah, I was feeling the whole look. He was clean shaven, with smooth skin. His physique was nice. I could tell he kept his body tight. He probably was a regular at the gym. Also, he had on some nice jewelry. Yeah, he wasn't bad at all. His clothes were put together well, too. I loved linen, and he was rocking a really nice linen shirt. He seemed to think he was all that. I didn't mind. I liked a man with confidence, as long as he had something to be confident about.

His girl was Dominican. She wasn't a bad looking girl, just a little plain with potential. Her hair was shoulder length and she had a nice smile. I could tell she pretty much let him run things. That was cool with me. It wasn't my business.

The poor woman was so nervous. I sat down and explained the entire procedure, and as I did with all my clients, I asked her a series of questions.

"Why do you want to have your butt done?"

"I want to look nice in my clothes and fill my pants out better. Also, when I go with Marvin to the strip club I like the way those girls' butts look," she answered.

In the middle of our conversation, Marvin interrupted. "Yeah, I want it rounded off at the top with a nice cuff at the bottom. Make sure it has a nice natural look because—"

I cut him off. "Excuse me. Are you having your butt done or is she? I'm confused because you have more to say than she does." *My goodness!*

Never had I experienced anything like this. I tried to ignore him and direct my questions to her, but that didn't matter. He wasn't backing down.

Every time I asked her something, she'd answer first, but then he'd follow up with his own answer and another question to go along with it. And to top it all off, he had the audacity to try and negotiate a better price. He was getting on my nerves so bad, I knew without a doubt they would be paying the regular price.

"How long will everything take? Did you ever have your butt done? How many times did you do it? How long did you have to wait between your sessions? How long ago did you have it done? I bet your boyfriend likes it."

I could understand a man coming to show support for his woman, but damn! I never heard someone ask more questions than the client. It threw me off a little because I figured it should have been her asking all the questions, not him.

"Trust me. My girl knows that I love women with big butts," he said.

I thought, *Hmm, now I know why she really wants her butt done.* I was about to tell her that I never agreed with anybody getting injections for someone else. The only reason I went through with the procedure that day was because they traveled so far and had paid for the hotel already. That wouldn't be right.

Out of the blue he told me, "You know, you're a pretty, chocolate lady."

"Thank you," I said, thinking his complimenting me like that in front of his girl was inappropriate, but hey, she didn't say anything, so neither did I. I just let it go.

During the procedure, I noticed how attentive he was to her. She was having a difficult time dealing with the pain from the injections. He came over to the table and held her hand, caressing it, and telling her she would be okay.

The whole time she kept saying she wasn't ever coming back. "This is it!"

Marvin and I laughed after I explained I'd heard that thousands of times. Chile, please!

He kept telling her, "It's almost done, just calm down." He watched the procedure from start to finish, and as if he had seen this before, he told her she needed to come back one more time. I didn't tell her, he did. All I could do was laugh to myself as I thought, *Wow, this dude is really something else.*

Finally, I told her, "Sweetheart, you make up your own mind. If you wanna come back, you call me."

He said, "She'll be back. She knows what I want."

Chapter 26

Nobody's Fool

Marvin's girlfriend's injections were tiresome. Not from working on her butt, but from Marvin himself. Less than thirty minutes after I left, he called me.

I was surprised to hear from him so quickly. But I must say, he wasn't rude or even flirtatious. He just expressed that they were very satisfied, and she wanted to schedule an appointment to see me again. I smiled.

He asked if I minded coming to their area the next go round. They lived in DC. I didn't have enough clients in that area to be traveling there regularly. The closest city I worked in was Baltimore, and I didn't go there frequently. However, in the next two weeks I'd be in New York and New Jersey. He agreed to meet me in New Jersey.

About a week later, Marvin called me. He just wanted to make small talk. Again, he wasn't flirtatious or anything, just making general conversation. But I ain't nobody's fool. I knew what he was up to. I just let him go ahead with his tactics. I wasn't dating anyone, and it didn't bother me. Besides, I didn't take him serious anyway. It was strictly for entertainment purposes only. I knew one thing though, I felt for his girl, but he was her problem not mine.

His girl and I were not friends. She was a client I met through him, and we had a business relationship. I didn't really feel any way about talking to him. It did make me think about what I already was feeling: "Men are something else and are not to be trusted."

A few weeks later, I met them in New Jersey. I brought along one of my guy friends from New Jersey. We were in the car together because we planned to hang out while I was in town. Our relationship was purely platonic, and we would just hang out from time to time. Nothing serious.

I asked my friend to stay in the lobby until I was done. Since I was going to work, there was no way I could have him come up to the room with me. It was bad enough that Marvin was there.

Within a few minutes of leaving my friend, I went up to Marvin and his girl's room so I could do her second set of injections. Marvin's girl's butt had not really changed that much. I only saw a little bit of a difference. Her butt had a square shape to it, so it was a little difficult to round out. But that wasn't unusual. Many women had that shape. I was just going to have to take my time to shape her.

Honey, Marvin was so happy to see me. Both he and his girl gave me a big hug. I was just like . . . "Wow!" He stepped back and looked at me from head to toe.

I thought, *Interesting.*

Before I got started, I told them my guy friend was waiting in the lobby, so I was going to be a little faster this time. I asked Marvin if he wouldn't mind going to keep him company so he wouldn't feel like he was waiting so long.

Baay-bee . . . let me tell you. The look on Marvin's face said, "Who do you think I am?" He didn't even respond, and acted as if I hadn't said anything to him. The energy in the room changed quickly. I didn't know if he thought that was beneath him or what. I couldn't read him. I thought Marvin would want to meet him, especially since on the few occasions that we talked, he was trying to tell me what kind of man I needed to be dating. Now he could go and have a look for himself, and see the type of company I was keeping. I kept making small talk, and he completely ignored me. Oh, okay, now I knew what was going on. He couldn't even hide what was on his mind if he wanted to. I didn't know if his girl noticed and just didn't say anything, or maybe she was too focused on the injections, but I certainly noticed. He was jealous! Marvin was a trip, and the entire situation was very awkward.

The first time, he was super attentive to his girl as she endured the agonizing pain. This time, homeboy was mute. In fact, I barely even knew he was in the same room with us. He didn't go meet my friend as I suggested. Instead, he sat quietly watching the television.

"Oh, his feelings are hurt or maybe his ego," I said to myself and set out to taunt him. I started talking a little loud to his girl to make sure he wouldn't miss what I was saying.

"Girl, I'm almost done. I don't mean to rush, but I gotta get back to my boo, so he can finish spoiling me."

"I hear ... ouch ... that," she said between injections.

"Yes, he took me to this wonderful intimate restaurant in NYC last night. He is so doggone sexy." I could feel the cloud of tension growing thicker around Marvin with every word I spoke. His girl was lying face down, so she couldn't see the look on his face, but I could. And if looks could kill, I know I would have been dead! Of course, I wasn't telling the truth, but it was making Marvin mad, so I just played the game. Why not have some fun?

When I was done, I could see that her butt was finally taking some form. I patted myself on the shoulder and thought, *Damn, you are a bad sister with that needle.*

I called my friend to let him know I was on my way down. I said, "Hey, babe, I just finished and will be down in a minute."

Marvin rolled his eyes. I looked at him and smiled.

Afterward, I went into the bathroom to wash my hands. The bathroom was located behind a separate partition, in a different part of the room. I finished up, and when I turned to walk away, I bumped right into Marvin. He tried to kiss me! I turned my head and gently pushed him away.

His girl was only a few feet away lying on the bed.

"Are you serious?" I whispered, in complete shock.

"Does it look like I'm serious?" he replied.

I walked away. I should've known Marvin was going to be a problem. Here he was with his girl, lying on the bed and just finished going through terrible pain to look good for his trife ass! Yet, he was focused on trying to get with me. See why I always stressed never get the injections for a man? I walked back into the room, got my money, and said my goodbyes as though nothing ever happened. The nerve of Mr. Marvin!

It took a few days for him to call me again. I was so busy I didn't even give what happened between us a second thought. I guess he was into his feelings, but oh well. He had someone at the time, and I wasn't interested in anybody else's man. I really didn't plan on dealing with him, so I wasn't concerned about whether he called. But boy, he started being so persistent.

As the weeks went on, I started taking his calls. When he finally calmed down and was out of his feelings, we had a decent conversation. I guess I can say we started to build a friendship. I never gave a second thought about what transpired in the bathroom at the hotel. It was irrelevant. I was on a mission, and Marvin was definitely not a part of that mission.

He always wanted to know why I wasn't dating anyone. I told him that my focus wasn't there. I hadn't met the right guy yet that held my attention. Besides, I got bored easily in relationships because the men I met were selfish. Yes, I wanted to date. I wanted to be vulnerable without being taken advantage of. To be able to cry without being charged as emotional. I wanted a man for more than just sex. I wanted to be submissive without anyone thinking I lacked substance. I wanted to cook for "him." Hell, I liked to cook. I even wanted to hold "his" hand while he took charge. But since I hadn't met anyone that I could share that with, I continued to stay focused on what was important to me right then.

Marvin would tell me that I hadn't met the right one yet. I didn't argue with that. At the time, I was letting the chips fall where they may, and I was okay with not being in a serious relationship. Relationships took time, and at that stage in my life, I didn't want to make the time. Let me rephrase that, I had the time if it was right. I just didn't want the negative energy that can come with it. I was doing me, and I was okay with that.

Once I was in New York, he was calling me back to back. I grew tired of sending him to voice mail, so I finally answered. We were talking, and he claimed he could barely hear me.

"All I hear in the background is noise and cars. Where are you?" Marvin asked.

"I'm in New York City!" I replied.

"How long are you going to be there?"

"I don't know, a couple of days. Why?" I asked.

"I'm taking the last train in, and I'm going to stay the night." He said it so casually, I assumed he already had plans.

"Really? Oh, okay, that sounds like fun. Where are you staying? Are you coming for a play or going shopping?" I asked out of curiosity. I knew DC wasn't that far, and it wasn't out of the norm for people to come down on the train for a day or weekend trip.

"No silly, I'm coming to see you. I planned on staying with you."

I didn't say anything.

"Umm hmm," I finally said. Again I grew quiet for a second or two.

"Hello. You still there?" he asked, breaking the silence.

"I'm here. I couldn't hear what you said. Let me call you back in a few when I can hear you better."

I ended the call. And no, I didn't call him back. I didn't have time to play with Marvin. He was doing too much and moving a little too fast. Who did he think he was? Or better yet, who did he think I was? I danced to the beat of my own drum, not his. Besides, he had a woman.

One of my friends that lived in New York was with me while this was going on. As soon as I ended the call, I told her what happened. She cracked up and told me I had a stalker on my hands. I played it off, because I knew what it was. It was all about the chase. Cat and mouse. Men loved the chase, and I was the one to give it to him. He called a couple of more times, but I sent him straight to voice mail.

Later, my friend and I had lunch and hit up Bergdorf Goodman's. I couldn't leave New York without getting my shop on. There were too many upscale stores and boutiques not to. It was a must.

The next day Marvin called and asked why I never called him back. I simply told him I got busy and it slipped my mind. He probably knew I was lying, but oh well. I didn't care. He would get over it. That still didn't stop him from continuing to dial my number. Some days I would answer and some days I wouldn't. It depended on my mood. This went on for about two months. He would call me, and I would speak to him briefly. Nothing more.

I'll never forget the day I finally gave in. I was in Baltimore working. It was a busy time because it was football season and the city was bustling. I got bored one night and called him. There wasn't much to do in Baltimore, and I grew tired of sitting around in my hotel room. I didn't know Baltimore too well, but I knew it was close to D.C. That same evening, I started feeling a little lonely and wanted to get into something.

He answered, upset of course, once I told him that I was in Baltimore. He wanted to know why I would come so close to him and not let him know I was there.

I ignored the question and his little attitude. I told him where I was staying and honey, I could swear he dropped the phone and was at my hotel room instantly. Marvin was at the football game, but left immediately to come see me. He knocked on the door, and I let him in. Honey, the rest is history, not necessarily good history though.

Chapter 27

Unnecessary Enemy

In 2004, I started traveling to New York and New Jersey often because my clientele really started to grow in those areas. I usually wouldn't travel to any state unless I had a minimum of ten clients. Otherwise, I felt it wasn't worth it. By the time I paid for airfare, hotel accommodations, and transportation, anything less than that felt like too much trouble. I tried to stay home with the kids as much as possible.

Before I left to go on a business trip, I always shipped my supplies overnight. The silicone, syringes, needles, everything I needed, would be waiting for me at the hotel. This way, I wouldn't have to travel with anything other than my personal things.

There in New York I befriended a client by the name of Lisa, who seemed like a really nice young lady, and I'd linked up with her several times while in New York. I didn't involve her in any of my business affairs. I really used her to take me places. Transportation in New York was so expensive, and flagging down taxis sometimes was a headache when I was trying to get from place to place. She didn't have much money, but I knew how bad she wanted my services. Lisa had injections done once, and that was just enough to make her want more, but she couldn't afford it. So we made a deal. I would barter with her for services.

In exchange for her running errands and driving me around, I would do her injections for less than half the normal price. She was very grateful for that and seemed happy with our little setup. I looked at it as a win-win situation for us both. It's not always about money, sometimes it's just about people helping each other out. I was always down for that. In this situation, she was benefitting more than me because I could have hired a car service and still saved. But like I said, it wasn't about that.

One particular time when I was in New York, I asked her to take me to New Jersey so I could get my lashes done. I was very meticulous about my lashes. Not just anyone could do them because I liked the natural look. It was worth the trek across the bridge.

Lisa picked me up and took me, no problem. She waited for me, and then we drove back to my hotel in Manhattan. Before she pulled off she told me she needed to ask me a favor. Lisa wanted to know if I could give her some injections. At the time I didn't see what the favor was; that was already part of our agreement.

"I'm strapped for cash right now. Miss Kim, I can't even pay the discounted fee," Lisa explained.

"Sorry, I can't do it this trip, but I promise I got you on the next trip," I said plainly. It had nothing to do with the fact that she didn't have the money. My silicone fluids were low. I had already been in New York for a couple of days working, and I only had enough to do one more person. My last client had a set appointment, and I didn't want to lose that money. Lisa could wait. I didn't tell her all that because I didn't feel the need to. I just told her I would do it the next time. No money or money. Yes, she could wait. I figured Lisa would understand, and since she didn't have any money she wouldn't mind waiting a few weeks.

Boy was I mistaken! This lady went off on me. She was pissed. But I couldn't understand why she was so upset when I still was going to hook her up later. She didn't see it that way at all. Lisa was talking reckless, and I was really tripping because I couldn't believe this. All over the injections. She acted as if I told her I was never coming back to New York. She knew I came there about every three to four weeks. Wow! Damn, I guess while she was driving home she got the balls of a giant. She called me on the phone talking plenty of shit.

I have never, *ever*, been the type of person to let anyone talk crazy to me. I was 38-Hot (my description for being pissed off), and I gave it to her just like she did me. I don't know who she thought she was talking to.

Unfortunately for me, I couldn't let it slide or brush it off. She had the game twisted, knotted up, and some more things. Nobody was going to disrespect me and talk to me sideways.

That was my attitude at the time, but of course now that I look back, I realize that I should have defused the situation to keep down the tension. What I was doing was illegal, and I didn't need unnecessary enemies walking around. My pride got the best of me, and I didn't care about the logical side. I felt we were better than that. Big mistake on my part.

"Well, you better not even think about coming back to New York *or* New Jersey," she threatened.

"I know you aren't threatening me as good as I have been to you."

"You can call it what you want to. You heard what I said," Lisa answered with major attitude.

"Listen, you can take those threats and kiss my behind. Say what you want because I don't care about your threats!" I yelled, wishing I could have jumped through the phone on her. Once again, I was not thinking rationally.

I wasn't just mad; I was hurt. I hate when I go out of my way and a person flips on me. Especially since her butt was looking really nice and full. I did a good job on her. She was more confident and everything. I just don't know what it is about those butts that make people so crazy.

151

Months passed since the incident, and it was nowhere near the forefront of my mind. It was back to business as usual. An enemy left unchecked can be a very dangerous thing. Thinking about a situation only after it has festered into an issue can be detrimental.

As I explained before, all of my clients came by referral. Usually, the normal process was that the person recommending my services would call me and give me a heads up that they were referring someone. This way, when the person called, I was already expecting them. I knew the name and all. Ninety percent of the time, that's how it went.

This was important, especially after the close call with the reporter in Detroit. But that was a few years ago, and you would have thought I'd learned from the hazards of getting too comfortable. Once again, I got caught slipping.

I got a call from a lady by the name of Kay in New York asking about making an appointment to get injections. She said she couldn't remember the name of the person who referred her. I didn't make any quarrels about it, but I should have. I just took her information and said I would let her know when I'd be back in New York. Since I had all my clients grouped together by city, I would just send her a text when I was on the way there.

If a client wasn't interested in seeing me, they just ignored the text, or sometimes they'd text back that they weren't coming, but they had someone else who wanted to come. That's what happened the majority of the time. They knew how secretive I was.

Kay called me, responding to my text. She wanted to know if she could meet me at 11:00 p.m. I agreed. Although it was late as I don't know what, I still agreed to it because I was late arriving myself.

Usually, I'd arrive at my designated city between 12:00 p.m. and 2:00 p.m. But this particular day I didn't get to New York until 6:00 p.m. It was a crazy day. Had I paid attention, I would have seen it as an omen.

I missed my original flight, which was definitely a sign that I shouldn't be going. But you know how that goes, everything is always clearer in hindsight.

Another sign I ignored was when I got to the hotel and my package holding the supplies hadn't arrived yet. I always sent my supplies via two-day delivery, and here it was the third day and no package. Just great! Usually, it would be waiting on me, but not today.

It was a disastrous day. The worst part was when I got there I had about twenty clients that had scheduled with me, and I couldn't service any of them. I was really pissed, but had I been able to read the future, I would have rejoiced. All of those setbacks turned out to be a blessing in disguise. I just couldn't see it then.

Chapter 28

Bad Vibes

The entire day was stressful. I hated having to reschedule everyone, but I didn't have a choice. Sometimes things just don't go as planned. I didn't have any supplies, so you already know I was too through.

I scheduled some people, including Kay, for later that night. It was messed up because that didn't pan out either, and I ended up having to reschedule her again. I was so stressed out, that when some clients called, I ignored them. That was not my style, to ignore a customer, but I didn't want to impose my mood on them. I always tried to be professional. My vibe wasn't right and I was off my square. I was frustrated and tired of explaining what happened repeatedly. It wasn't their fault, but you know how it can be.

The next day, I was able to get most of my clients done. Kay didn't come until about ten o'clock that night because I scheduled her last.

A little after ten, she showed up with another lady and introduced her as her friend. They were both Caucasian. Kay was a petite lady. She couldn't have been bigger than a size five or six. She had a cute pixie haircut and was dressed modestly. Her friend was bigger. I'd say about a size ten, with short hair and big eyes.

They took a seat and we began talking. Immediately, I got this strange feeling. I searched myself for some reason to be hesitant, but I couldn't put my finger on it. Erroneously, I just chocked it up to everything that had happened over the last twenty-four hours. Since I couldn't place it, I ignored it, and I can tell you now that I shouldn't have. But one thing I remember is that I definitely felt weird that day, all day. I couldn't explain it, but it was real.

I remember exactly what I was wearing: denim skirt, Uggs on my feet, and some camouflage leggings. I was dressed comfortably. The silicone fluid was on the table in a liter water bottle. Usually, I shipped the silicone in water bottles to keep it from leaking while being transported.

Kay looked around the room and began asking all kinds of questions.

"Uh, what are your prices?"

"The price starts at $800 and goes up in increments of $200, depending on the amount of cc's requested," I explained.

"What is the maximum amount I can get in one session?"

"I never inject more than 720 cc's in one session. In my opinion that amount is safe and decreases the chances of migration."

"Do you have any medical training?"

"No, and I will not lie about something so important. This way, any decision made by you after I let you know is totally up to you. I want you to have an opportunity to evaluate your decision fairly. I've never worked in the medical field."

The questions continued. I welcomed the questions, but I must say that I was surprised that more clients didn't take the time to ask so many questions. It was the right thing to do. Since it was so rare that anybody ever did ask such things, it was a little strange, too.

"How long is the recovery period?" Kay continued her inquiry.

"You need to stay off your butt for eight to ten hours. After each injection, I will place a cotton ball over the needle mark and stick it on with a glue gel. This will avoid the silicone from leaking out."

"Why eight hours?" she asked.

"Because it takes the body approximately eight hours to make a scab over the needle hole," I informed her. I went on to tell her the proper way to massage her butt the next day to avoid getting any lumps.

She seemed a little antsy but ready to get started after I explained everything. Before I started any procedure, I always took a good look at my client's butt, so I could determine exactly where to make the injections. Most clients were so anxious to take their pants off because that was the first step to them getting their new look.

"Okay, can you stand up and remove your pants?" I asked. Would you believe she said, "NO! I am too nervous. Can I please come back in the morning?" She looked as if she was about to jump out of her seat. Honey, I was too out-done.

"I need to see your butt tonight," I insisted.

"I don't want you to see my butt," she challenged. Her face turned beet red.

"Oh, okay, not a problem." Honey, at that moment, every alarm and warning bell was going off in my head. I knew something wasn't right with this. Who comes to get their butt done, but doesn't want me to see it? Even if she did want to come back later, this was equivalent to a consultation. Oh no! It was definitely time for me to get the hell up outta there.

I politely played it off. "Well, that's okay. We can do it another time. It is kind of late." I tried my best to hide my nervousness, because really, I was a nervous wreck. I was focused on one thing. Yes, that's right, leaving!

"Well, when do you think you will be ready?" I asked without giving away the fact that I was shaking in my Uggs.

"I can come back in the morning at eight o'clock," she agreed.

I put on my jolly happy face. "Okay, I'll see you then." But in reality, I was sweating in my boots, baby. And you know the fur in those Uggs didn't help. Kay practically ran out of the room.

As soon as I let them out, I packed my stuff in 2.2 seconds. I was out of there so fast, even I couldn't believe it. Immediately, I checked out of that hotel and checked into another. I could not sleep and I tossed and turned all night. I just knew they were undercover police.

At the crack of dawn I was up and at the airport. I made it to the airport by 5:30 in the morning and was on the plane by 6:45 a.m. By 10:15 a.m., I was back in Atlanta, eating breakfast with my eldest son, trying to breathe and calm down so I could get my nerves right.

My son and I were enjoying our breakfast. My phone began to ring and I jumped. That's when I knew my nerves were frayed. My son asked, "Mom, what is wrong with you?"

"Nothing, son. The phone startled me!" I calmed down and looked at the caller ID. It read: UNAVAILABLE. I ignored it the first time, but when it rang a second time, I decided to answer it.

"Hello?"

"Yes, is Kimberly Smedley available?"

"Who's calling?" I asked nervously. My heart was beating so loud, I believed she could hear it.

"I am calling from the *New York Post*. I want to know if I can ask a few questions. Is this Kimberly?"

I held the phone, contemplating what to say and she started in.

"Look Kim, we know you were in town last night and you checked out." My mouth hit the floor, honey. I gathered my composure and calmed down. I already knew the *New York Post* was a sleazy newspaper. Just like the *National Enquirer*, they were known for stretching the truth. She tried to get me to talk about the injections.

"I don't know what you're talking about, but whatever you print better not have no lies in it!"

Of course, about a week later, my phone started ringing like crazy. Everybody I knew in New York and New Jersey was calling and telling me about the article in the *New York Post.* I went on the Internet and read the article for myself. It was a trip and I was pissed. Some of what it said was:

A shady Atlanta businesswoman armed with a gallon jug of silicone and syringes is offering to inject women seeking "J. Lo butts" in a Manhattan hotel room—an illegal and potentially lethal cosmetic treatment . . .

"I need to see your butt," Kimberly Smedley told a Post reporter posing as a customer last week in a suite at the Eastgate Tower Hotel on East 39th Street.

Smedley, a heavyset woman wearing camouflage pants and fake Ugg boots, then demanded $1,600 in cash to give nine injections to each cheek.

Sitting on a coffee table was a Poland Spring jug, which she claimed contained "medical grade-silicone," along with a syringe and cotton balls.

"It's illegal," she said. "I'm not a doctor, and I'm not a nurse."

The article went on to say: ". . . *The Food and Drug Administration approves its [silicone] use to treat detached retinas but not for cosmetic purposes."* It also included a quote from a cosmetic surgeon who stated, *"Reputable plastic surgeons insert butt implants or do fat transfers—procedures costing $5,000 to $10,000 each."* He described the amounts I required for my services as *"dirt cheap"* in comparison to a reputable cosmetic surgeon.

A portion of the article also asserted, *"... Experts also fear that criminal providers use industrial-grade silicone, which is widely available as lubricants or sealants—and may contain toxic contaminants..."*

Of course, I read the article and it disclosed all the things Kay and I discussed when we were at the hotel. Kay kept that part pretty much accurate. But I was still too through, because the article went on to talk about someone who became sick. If you didn't read the article carefully, due to the way it was printed, one might think I administered those shots that put someone's health at risk. That wasn't the case. The reporter ran two different stories together, opening the door for a false assumption.

That's not even what really got me vexed. She had the nerve to print in the article that I had on "fake" Ugg boots. Me? Really? I think not.

Eventually, I was able to confirm that my "so-called" friend, Lisa, had called the *New York Post*. She was so upset that I couldn't do her injections that day, that she became my enemy.

A client of mine who was friends with Lisa, called her and put her on the speaker phone so I could hear their conversation. I was happy I found out who the culprit was. She said I got what was due to me. When I heard that, I just shook my head and hung the phone up. Damn my circle of clients/friends was getting smaller and smaller.

Jamaica seemed like the perfect place to visit right then.

Chapter 29

Count Your Blessings

One thing I have always enjoyed is traveling. This is such a big world and it's meant for us to see it. God designed and created this beautiful planet for us, so why not enjoy all that he made?

There was nothing like traveling. It took me away from the turbulence of everyday life. I could just lie back and collect myself. One of my favorite places to visit was Jamaica. I started traveling to Jamaica back in 1996. I have been to many places in the Caribbean, but I find there is no place like Jamaica. It's just too tranquil. I took my kids there so much that they actually started to complain.

"Mom, is this the only place we're ever going to visit?" Of course, eventually, they developed the same love for Jamaica as I had. I'd been all over the Caribbean, but there was something in the air in Jamaica.

I worked really hard, so Jamaica was my treat after long, busy weeks. The flight was convenient because J.A. was only two hours and forty-five minutes from Atlanta. For the past two years, I'd been going there every six to eight weeks. And even that wasn't often enough. I would just relax and rejuvenate.

Trust me, doing what I was doing was very stressful. I always had to look over my shoulder and make sure I wasn't going into a dangerous situation. The whole thing could be exhausting, both mentally and physically. It's a job in itself to keep such a major part of your life hidden from most people.

Whenever I stepped off the plane, it felt like all that stress would pack up and go on vacation too. It was wonderful. I could just be myself. No clients trying to rob me. No reporters looking to get a major story from the details of my life. I didn't feel the need to wear expensive designer clothes, expensive jewelry, or any of that. Honey, I wouldn't even pack those items. It was just me, the mountains, rivers, and clear blue ocean. I'd walk around carefree in my inexpensive little sundresses and sandals. I just did me.

I met a driver and became very comfortable with him. Navarel was really cool. Whenever I was coming to town, I would call him and let him know what time my flight was arriving. He'd be right there to meet me at the airport. While I was in town, I'd eat some of the best foods with the locals. I can taste the curry and jerk chicken, dumplings, salt fish, jerk goat and all the delicious foods right now. I'd walk and shop with the locals, too. I was just very comfortable with Jamaican people, and I didn't have an ounce of Jamaican in me. Although, I got so relaxed with them, I almost felt like I was a native. They would call me, The Jamerican.

I took Marvin with me several times. He expected to just be doing tourist things. At first, he was very uncomfortable with the way I moved around the island so freely and familiar like. He was hesitant and tense, but that is because Marvin was in law enforcement. He got to see the ugly side of people more often than most. This caused him to be a lot more skeptical and distrusting of people.

He wasn't only this way in Jamaica; he was like this all the time. That was his general personality. Marvin was very protective, but that was okay with me though. It made me feel safe. The ironic thing was, that was really opposite of how I should have been feeling with him.

Jamaicans were some of the hardest working people I had ever seen. They had a rare work ethic that made anybody who watched them, give them their respects. I was so impressed, and often felt overly grateful for what I had at home. It humbled you tremendously. We take so much for granted. I felt the need to give back in some way. I started asking around about different shelters for children. My driver told me about this place called MY FATHER'S HOUSE, located in Montego Bay. I've always had a passion for helping children. That's why I always worked with them at my church.

Children are innocent and vulnerable. Many children who have issues or what we call "bad behavior" are really just reacting to their unfortunate circumstances. Sometimes the fact that children are our future escapes us. They really are, and it is important that we nurture and care for them. No child ever asked to be born.

I asked my driver to take me to this place in Montego Bay. It was about a half hour ride from the airport and the resort where I was staying.

Lawd have mercy, the drive there was so scary. In Jamaica, the roads are very narrow. There was a mountainside on my left and a thirty-foot cliff drop on the right. The locals know the roads, so they tend to drive fast and rough. Kind of like a taxi driver maneuvering through New York City. It's normal to them, but a tourist might feel sick at the end of the ride. I can't lie; I was praying the entire drive. It's funny, because in America, we drive on the right side of the road, and in Jamaica, like many other countries, their natives drive on the left. When going around a corner, it always feels like you can't see the other car. The effect is that it just pops up on you. Now add that to some rain, and the thirty-foot drop just a few feet away. Yes, it was definitely an adventure getting there.

Once we arrived, we almost couldn't get in. The shelter required prior reservations, but after conversing with security, they agreed to let us in. The director came down and met us at the gate. I explained that I was interested in the shelter, and I was visiting from the United States. She told me the shelter was founded by an organization called Mustard Seed in Atlanta, Georgia. I smiled because I knew that this had been divinely ordered.

Mustard Seed Communities serve over 500 children, young adults, and families from all over Jamaica. The population includes people with disabilities, children affected by HIV/AIDS, and teen mothers along with their babies. They also have a few different educational centers that focus on teaching and providing schooling for local populations. I thought the whole thing was profound, and it was so good to see that even though Jamaica has a lot of poverty, they still don't forget the little ones. The Mustard Seed program was a form of unity and also highly praise-worthy.

We were taken in to see the place. I must say, I was very impressed. I instantly fell in love with the work they were doing with the children.

One of the things that stuck out first was the cleanliness of the place. It was spotless. I couldn't believe it. A place swarming with children looked the opposite of what I expected. Usually, adults would have to run behind kids to clean up their mess, or get after them about cleaning up behind themselves. There was nothing out of place. Also, there wasn't any air conditioning, but that didn't deter the staff from working hard to run the place efficiently.

Many of the children there were disabled, so quite a few of them were still in diapers. Several of them had been abandoned by their parents because they couldn't afford to take care of them. There was one little boy who I will never forget. He stands out so vividly in my mind. His name is Michael. Little Michael was mentally challenged, but I don't remember exactly what his diagnosis was. All I know is that he was so handsome. He followed us around the entire time.

When it was time for us to go, he grabbed my hand and pointed toward the exit. He was unable to speak, so I didn't understand what he meant. I just kind of stood there for a moment. He pulled on my hand and tugged at me. Michael then pointed to himself and then me. He wanted to know if he was going with me. I can't describe how that touched my heart. All children want is a family and a mother to love them, and they all deserve to have that.

I asked the director about funding and what they received from the government. She explained that government funding was virtually non-existent. Ninety-five percent of their funding came from Mustard Seed and private donations. I learned that doctors who traveled there would sometimes bring medical supplies such as Tylenol and other cold medicines. They were in dire need of supplies.

I made sure to leave them with money the first day I went there. Every so often when I visited Jamaica, I made sure I did something for that shelter. Even if it was just buying pampers and medicine. I'd make sure it got to them. I will never ever forget that place.

So many of us are fortunate, even in the situations that we think are complicated or difficult. Visiting a place like that makes you re-define your definition of poor. There is always someone worse off than you, so remember to count your blessings.

Chapter 30

The Big Butt Phenomenon

Question: If the media didn't put such a huge emphasis on butts, would the phenomenon be as big as it is today? Would the desire for a large butt fade out like afros or bell bottoms? I'm not sure, but I think the question is worth asking. I can remember a time when big booties were (just) attractive. Now, they are like a status thing, almost a requirement.

Big butts are all over music videos and talked about in hip-hop lyrics regularly. The rapper 2Chainz has a song and the hook goes, "All I want for my birthday is a big booty girl!" Go just about anywhere, and you can hear little girls, teenage girls, and even grown women singing the lyrics to songs like this one, amongst other things.

This creates an expectation of what women think they need to look like. It's not just the girls, but the boys too. They get introduced to the idea that a man should have a woman with a big ol' booty. It creates expectations on both sides, especially in black society.

The result is dissatisfaction with yourself when you look in the mirror and don't see what you hear your favorite rapper describing. He might have said big this and big that is what looks perfect, but you may not see that when you look at yourself. We start to value ourselves based on things that really aren't important. Maybe if we ponder the hidden costs of this kind of thinking, we'll see the real issues lurking behind it.

There is no such thing as a quick fix to repair damaged self-esteem. Anytime you are willing to risk your health to satisfy your desire for a bigger butt, bigger cheeks, bigger lips or what-have-you, there are deeper issues than any silicone can ever fix. There are internal feelings that need to be first admitted, then dealt with. We can't begin to fix a problem if the individual with the problem hasn't accepted they even have one. Once we realize we do have a self-esteem issue, then we can start to address the source of our ill thinking. Oftentimes, we don't think there is anything wrong with us, so we can't start repairing the damage, nor can we even address the problem directly.

I am not exempt from this. Once, I undervalued myself too. I never would have admitted that self-esteem issues were the root of my desire for a bigger butt. If anybody would have tried to convince me that, that was the case, I would have argued them down, honey. Not me. I would have looked at them and said, "I only want a bigger butt because it's sexier, more appealing, and more attractive than a pancake booty." Right? . . . Wrong!

The truth was, I was insecure because I let other people's concepts of beauty warp and distort the love I had for myself. When I was going to those clubs and wearing outfits that covered myself so others couldn't see my butt, that meant I valued my butt more than myself as a whole. Now had I been out there loving myself regardless of how my butt was shaped, and then decided to get the injections, that would be quite different. Because my butt's shape wouldn't have taken away from me enjoying life. It would have just been something I did to enhance it. But when something so minor actually causes you to miss out on some of life's gifts, there is definitely something going on inside.

Not everyone who changes something about themselves has self-esteem issues. As I said, it's about the mindset of the individual before they have any alterations.

Culturally, sometimes physical changes identify who we are. In Indonesia, there is a tribe called "Mentawai" where the women shave their teeth into sharp triangular points. There is no anesthesia. It's so painful and done only to the women. The sharper the teeth, the more attractive they are to their prospective husband.[4]

Many tribes in Africa cut into the skin on their arms, face, or neck, a process known as tribal marking. This sometimes signifies puberty, or tells which specific tribe you are from, or if you're married or eligible. It's seen as attractive to some and even honorable.

Circumcision amongst boys usually occurs at birth. It is a painful mutilation of their penis, cutting off the foreskin. This is skin that contains thousands of nerve endings that can bring immense pleasure to a man. Yet it is cut off when they are so young, that they have no way to make that decision themselves, regardless if whatever the reason the parent has decided to do so. However, if a parent chooses not to circumcise their son, once that boy realizes that he doesn't have a circumcised penis like most others, they may feel like they need to get it done. Not because of their religion or health, but simply because it may be the "norm" in their society.

I remember watching an episode of Oprah, and she featured these women on her show from a country in Northwest Africa called Mauritania. If a woman was too skinny, she became an outcast. Even sometimes ridiculed. The bigger the woman, the more attractive she was.[5] And honey, I'm not talking about just a little thick. I'm talking about down-right fat.

Little girls were overfed purposely to fatten them up. This was done to ensure that they would find a husband because that was the way women were expected to look in their culture. I imagine that a girl with a very high metabolism might go to extremes to try and maintain her heavy weight status for acceptance purposes.

As women from all around the globe, we endure so much. The expectations thrown at us, pushing us to try and be as attractive as possible, usually does more damage than it does anything else.

We are always going to see the differences between ourselves and others. And that is okay. Sometimes, however, we need to detach ourselves from the outside influences and expectations other people put on us. Especially when they are just physical and not health related. If we are always pleasing others, responding, reacting, and changing in order to satisfy the will of others, we lose ourselves. Our beautiful, precious, one-of-a-kind selves are priceless. There is nothing worth losing that.

Instead of being creative, we'll be copying or imitating all the time. As they say, "Love the skin you're in."

Chapter 31

Motor City Incidents

Detroit, Motor City, or The "D." Whatever you wanna call it, is one of my favorite places to go. Whether it's clubbing on Woodward, walking Belle Isle, or gambling at the casino, I found my way around. In the summer I even attended concerts at Chene Park, where they would have some well-known artists. We took blankets, drinks, and food and just chilled. I loved going there. Of course, business was very good to me in Detroit. Those strippers were dedicated to mastering their craft.

One of my stripper client's, Lush, was a pretty girl with a really cute shape. She had a little butt and it was round already. She just wanted it filled out and plumper. Lush came to me by a referral from another girl I'd worked on, who sent several people my way. I met her at her hotel room and she was so excited.

I set up a makeshift operating table and told her to lie on her stomach. She explained that she wanted the maximum amount of cc's she could get in one session.

Like always, I explained the process so no client is shocked by the pain. She said she could handle it, so I got started. Baay-bee, let me tell you, honey. That chile was screaming so loud, you would have thought I was pulling her tooth.

"Oh my God!" Lush shrieked. She moved, causing me to pull the needle out.

"You have to be still," I told her, trying to finish. But almost an hour had passed, and I barely got anywhere. She was hollering and flapping around like a fish. I kept telling her to quiet down because I was expecting hotel security to come knocking on the door at any moment. It sounded like somebody was being tortured, and normally I would stop the procedure because it would be too much. I didn't like all the chaos and the theatrics.

Finally, I finished the first butt cheek and didn't know if I'd be able to keep her calm through the second cheek, or if I should charge her extra for having me on my feet for two hours when the job took only a half hour normally.

She calmed down some and I started on the next side. I stuck the needle in and before I knew it, home girl jumped off the table hollering. Luckily, I was able to pull the needle out, but the fluid was leaking from her butt. I stared at her with a straight face. At this point I wasn't able to inject anymore. I sealed the hole and told her, "Get up." After dealing with the drama, I was tired and frustrated.

"I can't do it. I'm sorry. It's hurting way too bad," she said. "Can you numb it?"

"I really don't like to numb. The topical numbing cream doesn't stop the pain. The needle going in isn't what hurts. It's the actual fluid going in that hurts." I tried injecting numbing medicine before I started the actual procedure. But I later learned from a doctor in the Dominican Republic that numbing medicine is a nerve blocker, and that, mixed with silicone made the procedure more of a health risk.

"But you have to finish. We already did one side," I explained. One of her butt cheeks looked significantly larger than the other.

"I don't care," Lush said. Home girl actually got dressed and was leaving. I kept trying to tell her that her butt looked crazy, but she was not trying to hear me. "I'm not getting back on that table."

I couldn't believe it. I just had this dumbfounded look on my face. She walked out of there with one full butt cheek, and when she closed the door, I fell out on the couch laughing. For a while I waited, thinking she would come back after she calmed down. But she never did. A few days later, she called asking if I was still in town. She came with three of her friends. One held her hands, one held her legs, and one put a towel in her mouth. I just wanted to finish what I started. Do you know after all of that she asked when I would be in town again. I told her, "Never!"

Another referral came to me from a stripper in Detroit. It was an unusual referral because it was a man. Yes, a man, and she said he was a regular at the strip club and spent a lot of money on her. She bragged about how much money he would drop.

I had serious reservations. Especially since I didn't work on men anymore. For one, I was turned off after damn near breaking my arm when I was injecting transvestites. Their muscles were just too dense. Secondly, like I said before, I didn't feel right in my spirit trying to give a man breasts or making him look like a woman. Last, but not least, I wasn't trying to get robbed. I could hold my own in a girl on girl brawl, but I was no competition for a man who might try and hurt me. I wasn't too anxious to do it.

She kept pressing me though, and she was a good client. After a lot of persuasion, she finally convinced me to meet him. I agreed, but Marvin had to be there. I was staying at the MGM in downtown Detroit. I only stayed at nice hotels because it was important for both my clients and me. I did not want them to ever come see me to get injections at a place where I wouldn't lay my own head. Some of my competition would take their clients to cheap hotels and motels and that was just so tacky to me. My clients spent good money for their services. I wanted to make sure they had some comfort, even though the procedure could be painful for some.

I felt safer in big hotels, and I think it made my clients feel safer too. It spoke volumes about the type of person I was.

Anyway, so this guy and my client who referred him came to see me. His name was Nathan. He was very sexy. Nathan was half Greek and half Italian. He wore his hair in a long ponytail, stood about 5-feet 10-inches tall, and was dressed metro-sexual. He had a very sexy build. Thick thighs and flat abs. Just the way I liked my men. He definitely could turn heads. Nathan was simply gorgeous.

"Hello, Miss Kim. It's a pleasure to meet you," he said charismatically.

"Same here," I said, smiling. My goodness, he was *hot*!

"I have my own room a few floors up." I was happy to hear that. He was very poised, mannerable, and classy. The woman with him was pretty. I looked at her and remembered her from a couple of years back. She was always quiet and reserved. Her body was banging, and she never seemed like the average strippers that I'd met. We all went up to his room. You know I had to start with the questions.

"So what is it you want me to do for you?" I asked. If he wanted his penis done, I'd be referring him elsewhere.

"I want to do my butt," Nathan said. I tried to hide my look of shock and went on to ask him other questions.

"Why do you want your butt done?" I asked. The same as I asked any other client.

"Well, I have a butt fetish. I absolutely love a nice butt. I want to be able to look back and see my butt poking out in my jeans."

Marvin turned his head. I could tell he was disgusted, and I tried my best to keep a straight face, but in my head I was thinking, "What in the world!"

"What kind of look are you going for?"

"I want my butt to look like Dwayne Johnson's."

"Who?" I asked.

"You know . . . The Rock." I was quiet for a moment before I responded.

"Ohh-kay!" In my mind I was thinking, *I guess. Whatever!* "So what do you do for a living?" I just knew he was an exotic dancer or something like that.

"I'm an emergency room doctor."

"Wow!" I was shocked. You just never know. So I gave him the price, and I told him to pull his pants down and lie across the bed. Honey, when he pulled his pants down he had on a pair of pantyhose with a red thong. I couldn't believe it!

First of all, my client who was with him seemed like she wasn't surprised. I mean, she told me he wasn't gay. I asked her that before they came because I just assumed he was because he was a male coming to see me. She quickly corrected that and assured me otherwise. So you know the thong and pantyhose really had me tripping.

I just had to ask him, but I did it in a non-judgmental way.

"Ummm, one question, why are you wearing a thong and pantyhose?"

"Why? You don't like them?"

"Yes, I think they are cute, but why are *you* wearing them?"

"I love the way they feel on my skin," he said.

I didn't say anything. What could I say? He acted like it wasn't unusual.

I gave him what he came for and he was super satisfied. I started calling him Dr. Nathan.

After that first consultation, I saw Dr. Nathan often. If he wasn't coming to have something done on himself, he was bringing one of his many girlfriends. The girls were always beautiful. I'd do many of their butts. Eventually I had to cut Dr.

Nathan off from getting more injections. His butt was getting thicker than some of my female clients.

Sometimes the clients he referred would come alone if Nathan was working. He was always busy since he worked as an ER doctor in Lansing, Michigan. Lansing was about two hours outside of Detroit. I'd ask the girls questions about Dr. Nathan, like, "Are you sure he's not gay?"

I know, I know it wasn't my business, but Dr. Nathan was just so sexy. I couldn't understand why a straight guy would be wearing pantyhose and a thong! I just didn't get it. He dressed like a man, so he wasn't a cross dresser, just strange.

After getting his butt done, Dr. Nathan went home and modeled his new butt in a thong. Then he'd take pictures and text them to me. The text said: "Look how nice your work is." Chile, I deleted those pictures right out of my phone. I wouldn't even bother to reply.

Dr. Nathan and I ended up having a good relationship. He is one of the doctors that I talked to in-depth about what I was doing. Dr. Nathan was very insightful and gave me good information. We still keep in contact.

Chapter 32

Surprise! Surprise!

The saying, "All good things come to an end" is sad but true. At least for me. I remember when I got arrested. I flew in to DC to see Marvin because our relationship was already on thin ice. He wasn't happy that I had met someone, and I was trying to stay committed. About six weeks had passed since we last spoke, and now that I was dating someone new, Marvin and I didn't see eye to eye on many things. Probably because another man had my complete attention. And even though Marvin had someone else, it wasn't acceptable for him to know that I was dating someone. That was his way of thinking. So this trip was strictly for making up. I knew I still needed him around because he was my security, and I didn't want there to be any bad blood between us. I still cared about him, and part of me was looking forward to us making up. The whole thing unfolded so strange though.

Marvin picked me up from the airport. I was happy to see him. I don't know, but I missed not being around him. Six weeks was the longest I had gone without seeing him. For the past year and a half, we were together almost two to three times a week.

We went out to dinner. We laughed and drank. It felt like old times. I was really enjoying myself. He always had a way of making me feel good. Marvin was different from the guy I was currently dating. My current boyfriend was nice and treated me well, but I can't explain it; Marvin was just different.

We went to my hotel and I checked in. Once we were in the room, we started to get comfortable. Out of the blue, Marvin said he wanted to get me another drink. I didn't want anything else to drink because I was already feeling the effects of drinking during our meal. But he was so adamant about it and kept insisting I didn't argue. I thought, *Maybe that was his way of wanting some privacy to use the phone or something.* During the time we were together, I noticed he responded to a few text messages. I told him to go on.

He left the room while I was getting dressed for bed. I called my boyfriend and talked to him for a few minutes. I wanted to let him know I arrived in town safely. He thought I was in DC to work, and I didn't want him to worry in case he called and I didn't answer. Actually, he left me in Atlanta to go on a business trip himself, and that made it easy for me to go see Marvin.

Just as I ended my call, there was a knock at the door. I assumed it was Marvin returning. I thought, *That was quick. Or maybe he changed his mind or forgot something.* I looked through the peephole before opening the door. Just in case it wasn't Marvin, I needed to put on something.

I couldn't make out the faces and all I saw were badges. It looked like hotel security. I asked, "Who is it?"

"FDA, open up!" My heart began to race. They didn't say FBI. What did they want? Any name with three alphabet always made me nervous, but I calmed down and remembered I wasn't there for business. I was only with Marvin. I didn't have any silicone. So I convinced myself that it was no big deal, and I opened the door. They rushed in, showing their badges with their guns drawn. I was flabbergasted. So I raised my hands and stepped back. I'm sure they could hear my heart beating. They immediately wanted to know where the solution was. I had enough sense not to open my mouth. I didn't answer any of their questions. Instead, I sat on the bed and looked at them like I didn't understand anything they were saying. They continued to throw questions out there. I stayed quiet. There were about seven agents in total. I just couldn't believe it. Where the hell was Marvin? It's like time stood still.

They tore that room apart, but I didn't have anything but my purse and a small overnight bag. I planned on flying home the next day. They wanted to know who else was with me. The way they were asking was as if they already knew someone was with me. I told them yes, but the person wasn't armed.

After about fifteen minutes, which felt more like five hours, Marvin came back to the room carrying my Johnnie Walker Blue Label. I know I was complaining before about him getting the drink, but right about now . . . please! I really needed a drink. Marvin looked stunned by the uninvited guests. They turned their attention to him and began to ask questions.

He was very short with them and told them the same thing I said. I was only there for one night, solely to see him. Marvin was very professional and gave them one of his business cards. They looked at the card and asked what he did for a living.

"I own a security company. I'm a former DC police officer," he said.

I didn't know it at the time, but that statement would later be the biggest mistake he ever made.

Surprise, surprise. I didn't know the FDA could arrest me. But any federal agency from the Post Office to the IRS had a division comprised of agents who could initiate the arrest process. And yes, I was being arrested.

I told Marvin to call my son, Dave, and let him know I was being arrested. I wanted him to get in contact with my god brother who lived in Baltimore, so he could get me a lawyer. There were no words to describe what was going through my mind. Nervousness, fear, shame, embarrassment and so many other emotions. I had so many unanswered questions racing around in my head. I didn't know who told, or how they even knew about me. What was going on!

They let Marvin go, but handcuffed me. I asked them if I HAD to be taken out in handcuffs. That would have been the worst.

I always saw people on the news being arrested and holding their head down, or covering themselves in a shirt or towel to hide their identity. Now I fully understood why. It's horrible. I was really tripping about being walked through the hotel in handcuffs.

There was one female agent, and I think she felt bad for me. She arranged for a jacket to be put over my cuffs and for me to be taken out the back door. The agent even let Marvin take my purse and my jewelry. Still, the hotel workers saw me. I had such a good rapport with that hotel. I stayed there often, so the embarrassment was real. It was a very nice hotel, only two blocks from The White House.

They arrested me in DC, but took me to a jail in Baltimore. I guess it was a city or county jail where they locked up people who had just been arrested by the Baltimore Police Department. I was the exception to the rule because I wasn't 'property' of Baltimore; I was a federal inmate.

That distinction was made clear when I wanted to use the phone. I saw other women using the phone, so I asked if I could also. The arresting agent said he would ask the guards if I could make a call. I hadn't even been processed, and I was asking to use the phone. They said I couldn't, because I was a federal inmate. I had to be separated from the others.

The Feds, in some cities have FDC's or MDC's. That's a Federal Detention or Metropolitan Detention Center. They are pre-trial facilities operated by FBOP (Federal Bureau of Prisons) to house only federal detainees. If you end up getting arrested in a city that does not have a FDC, you get stuck at a county jail. The US Marshalls pay the county jails to hold their detainees during the court or pre-trial process. It sucks because you miss out on some of the amenities the federal government provides (if you can call them amenities!).

The agent processed me. You know: fingerprinting, mug shots, and all that. Then he said he'd be back to get me at 8:00 a.m. That meant I would definitely have a long night. He informed me that I couldn't get a bond without going before the judge because I was arrested by the Feds. I was so afraid because I knew a lot of times when you were arrested by the Feds you didn't get a bond. I looked around at the other women. OMG! I saw them picking their arms, necks, and faces. They were rocking back and forth. I can't deny it; I was terrified. It was like something out of a movie. What was wrong with them?

When the guard took me to the nurse to take my blood, I remember asking her why the women in lockup were acting so erratic. She explained that most of the women were on heroin, and they were going through withdrawal. I couldn't believe it. Although I'd heard that heroin addiction was bad in Maryland, this was the first time I'd experienced it up close. I started to feel sad. It was horrible. I wanted to go home. Never had I wanted to use the phone so bad in my life. I kept asking, but the guards ignored me.

Because I was a federal inmate, I was placed in a cell alone. It was cold. No, it was damn near freezing. They gave me two blankets and a pillow. The guard came in and put a mattress on the floor. None of the other prisoners had that. Some of the women were beating and banging on the glass asking how I received blankets and a pillow.

The guard shrugged his shoulders. "She's federal property." That's when I figured it was true what they said about the Feds: you got treated a little different if you were their property. I wouldn't necessarily say better, because there is nothing to glorify about being arrested. However, the county jails didn't want to lose their contracts with the Feds, so they tried to avoid complaints from their special guests.

The next morning the agent took me to the federal building and turned me over to the US Marshals. I was processed and fingerprinted all over again. Then I was put in a cell that resembled a cage with about fifteen other females. I was still asking to use the phone. I wasn't allowed. They said I had to wait until the pre-trial officer came to see me. From my position I could see other cages that were holding men. When the guards walked through, it looked like they were viewing animals. They took the men to court, but first they shackled them together around their feet and waist and they also placed black boxes with cuffs on their wrists. Oh no! I couldn't take it. Panic set in.

The day went by so slow. I kept asking the guards as they went by what time it was. It seemed like time was at a standstill. I was going nuts because I wasn't sure what was going on, and I didn't know if an attorney had been sent to see me or what.

The other fifteen women in the cell with me were charged with "Human Trafficking." The Feds had been watching them transport women from Texas to Maryland for months. Once you cross state lines doing anything illegal, it can become a federal matter. They were accused of forcing women to sell their bodies and travel from Texas to Maryland against their will. One woman was about eight months pregnant. At lunch time, we were fed bologna sandwiches with mustard and some terrible tasting orange drink. I gave mine to the pregnant woman.

I had never *ever* seen anything like it. The whole situation had me feeling very uncomfortable. Since I was a pre-trial detainee, a pre-trial officer came to see me. The pre-trial officer takes all your personal information and then makes a recommendation to the judge if you should be eligible for a bond release.

I thought I would really lose it when the pre-trial guy explained that I may not get to see the judge because of the human trafficking case. There were just too many people involved in that situation and not enough hours in the day. I immediately started to cry.

The only thing that calmed me down was the pre-trial officer telling me that when I did see the judge, I'd most likely be released on my own recognizance. That was definitely something that made me hopeful. After the interview with the pre-trial officer, I was put back in that dreaded holding cell.

I tried to get some rest. I was so exhausted. All I wanted was a hot bath. I still had on my clothes from the day before and my hair was a mess.

Around 2:00 p.m., I was taken to the front and told I had an attorney visit. I was so happy. Finally, someone had come to help me out of this mess. As soon as I saw him, I looked him up and down. I needed to make sure he was up to par.

My first words were, "Are you a paid lawyer or a public defender?"

"Paid," he replied.

I felt so relieved, and I didn't even ask who sent him. I just let out a sigh of relief. Thank goodness somebody did. I was so happy to see him, I could have kissed him. After my release, I found out the guy I was dating paid for my lawyer. Not Marvin. My son had called him and told him what happened. As soon as he heard, he jumped right on it.

The attorney explained that in the next half hour I'd be going into the courtroom to see the judge. He told me what to expect and how everything would go. He then told me I'd have to surrender my passport. Most people would be happy to know that they were going home, but honey, I had the nerve to cry. That's right. I was in tears because that meant no Jamaica, no Dominican Republic, no other place outside the U.S. That was just too much to take in.

When I got into the courtroom, I saw Marvin sitting all the way in the back. I looked at him and smiled. It felt good to know I had his support. Standing before the judge not knowing what was about to happen had me on edge. At least I thought I had his support.

Weary eyed and stressed, I stood before the judge. When he asked the US Attorney what I was being charged with and what amount of time I'd be facing if convicted, the US Attorney didn't even know. He had to do some research right there in the courtroom and go through the law book. The judge even wanted to see the information for himself. I guess he wanted to make sure it was the right application.

You see, they had never charged anyone with a crime like mine before. My case was setting a precedence. I couldn't be charged under medical malpractice because I wasn't a medical professional. But one thing I've learned is that if the Feds want you, they WILL make up a new charge, if they can't find one already in existence.

I went through my bond hearing and all the formalities that went with it. The judge agreed to release me on MOR (My Own Recognizance).

More than grateful, I left the courtroom with Marvin and got in the car. Immediately, I called my son Dave and let him know I was out. He said my boyfriend wanted me to call him. I didn't care that I was with Marvin. The Feds kept my cell phone, but I didn't care about that either. I used Marvin's phone and called my boyfriend. He didn't ask me any questions and was on point with me. One of his friends lived in Baltimore, and he wanted me to get to his friend ASAP. He didn't even say why. His friend met up with me and gave me a couple thousand to get back to Atlanta. I was left speechless.

Really, I felt bad. Here I was with Marvin, who didn't even offer to pay for a night at a hotel. Even though I had my own money, that wasn't the point. My new man had everything together and was right there in my corner, even though he wasn't physically with me. I felt like crap for cheating on him with Marvin. It wasn't even worth it.

That afternoon I checked into a hotel so I could leave in the morning. I was completely drained and couldn't wait to lie down in a comfortable bed. When I got to my room I took a long, hot bath and slept until the next morning.

There were so many unanswered questions. *Who told? How long had the Feds been watching me? Was it a client or competition?* I just didn't know. I flew back to Atlanta and I knew one thing . . . It was over!

Chapter 33
There's No News Like Bad News

There is no news that travels like bad news. I wasn't even home for a good thirty minutes before my phone started ringing off the hook. Clients from all over the country had been calling me. The Feds had seized my cell phone, and since my clients were all grouped by city, it was easy for them to know where all my busiest cities were. My arrest was on the news in Baltimore, DC, and Detroit. The Feds had a strategy. By putting my arrest on the news in various cities, they hoped they would get people to come forward to testify against me.

The news used pictures from my Facebook Page when running my story. I took that particular photo when I was out in Costa Rica. News spread like wildfire. The story was featured everywhere. Their strategy worked opposite of what they were hoping for. Most of my clients did pick up their phones, but it was to call me and make sure that I was okay.

I felt like my world was spiraling out of control. Everything was crashing down on me. The media was relentless. I told everyone who inquired about me that I was fine. I've always considered myself a very strong person, and that strength that I claimed was definitely being tested.

The next day, I started getting calls from *Media Takeout, The Washington Post, New York Post, The Atlanta Journal-Constitution* and so on. News of my arrest and my case were on the radio and all over the Internet. I was in a trance. It was surreal to me. I had no idea how all these people were getting my phone number. They were asking if I wanted to give my version of events. You know, the *backside of the story.* I was very tempted. They, however, would only twist my words to fit the message they wanted to sell. I would appear defensive, and there was nothing I could say that could help me. They were going to report, print, tell and tweet their own versions, regardless of anything I said.

Be it TV, radio, or social media, I was portrayed as a monster. We all know the media. If you watch the news daily, then just ask yourself when was the last time you saw anything positive. If you've ever dealt with the media, then you know exactly what I'm talking about. If it's not an act of heroism, then they tell *all* the bad.

They talked about (my) case, but then brought up another case. It was a state case somewhere and someone had died from injections or had lost a limb. But it had nothing to do with me. They were running different stories all into one big story, painting me out to be something I was not. It was looking like I did those things, and the defamation was really driving me crazy. There was an article in *Ebony* about a woman who'd lost all her limbs. Even though she never came forward and said who injected her, the media still found a way to try and tie it to me. They were ruthless.

It was difficult for me to sit and watch those things and not be able to do anything about it. We all have limitations, and when circumstances seem scary, our imagination runs wild. Mine definitely did. I was thinking all types of things. Relaxing in the midst of a crisis is something much easier said than done.

The media symbolically and literally is a giant. Their presence in any situation intensifies it dramatically. It's difficult to get your mental balance back, but you must, if you plan to go on living somewhat of a normal life and prevailing.

It got to the point where I had to completely cut out watching the news and listening to the radio. In Atlanta, a male radio personality dogged me out so bad, that it was beyond necessary. I wanted to call into his show and tell him, "You might be dogging me out right now, but your wife thinks the world of me. I'm the reason she walks around in camisoles with her butt sitting up pretty and wearing boy shorts to bed every night. You just don't know because she never told you. But you should be thanking me instead of trying to clown me!" That's what I really wanted to say. But I held my tongue. It made no sense to stoop to another person's level. Besides, I didn't want to put an innocent client on blast.

After the first call from the media, I contacted my attorney. He told me to tell anybody else who tried to get an interview from me to call him. I did just that. I referred all media people to my lawyer. I knew he'd handle them.

One day I was entirely too stressed. So I decided to call my masseuse over so I could get a good massage, hopefully to ease some of the tension and tightness I was feeling. As my masseuse tried to leave, my son came in the room and looked at me with a strange expression.

"What's wrong?" I asked him.

"Mom, there are reporters outside the house." The poor masseuse couldn't leave because I didn't want them to harass her. Also, I didn't want her to feel pressured to answer any questions.

My attorney, Steven Berne, wouldn't give anyone an interview. His reasoning made a lot of sense. When I asked him why not, he said, "Kim, there is nothing that can be said to help you right now. So why say anything at all. The circus will move on soon enough." He didn't see the point in entertaining any interviews. My one priority was trying to stay out of prison, and that was definitely my attorney's main focus.

The Backside of the Story

I started to receive many phone calls from several talk shows. Initially, I was up in the air about doing it. I actually considered it because I felt it would be different than talking to a regular reporter. They could see me and hear my side of the story directly. I felt my clients needed to know the truth. There were so many rumors and lies floating around; I wanted them to know that everything I told them was absolutely true. I thought about addressing it once and for all.

My lawyer did not agree. He stressed that what was truly important was my defense. "You can tell your story later," he said. Steven was absolutely right, because nothing good was going to come from that. He advised me not to talk to the media until I had something good to promote. Also, he explained that no matter what, they were going to throw me under the bus, and since that was going to happen regardless, I needed to have something positive to talk about.

To this date, he has only given one interview to the media, outside the courtroom the day Marvin testified. It was important because it confirmed that I was using medical grade silicone from a doctor. Of course, the media edited that part out. I saw firsthand what my attorney had been warning me about all along. They will print what they think will sell, even if it's not the truth.

Several producers approached me before I self-surrendered to Federal Prison Camp. They wanted to film my preparation for prison. My family and friends were stressed out enough, and I didn't want them going through anything extra just for a few extra dollars. It just wasn't worth it, not at all. I refused and I still feel it was the right decision.

When you feel like you are being attacked, sometimes you want to engage your attackers. It doesn't matter if you are in the right or in the wrong; it's human nature to want to protect

187

yourself. But that would have kept the fiasco alive. Instead, I humbled myself, admitted to my wrongdoings, and the media attention died down. It was hope for me that one day, maybe I could actually put all of this behind me.

Chapter 34

Talk About Double Standards

Okay, now what was really a trip was my family and friends finding out about my arrest and the facts surrounding it. To say they were shocked is an understatement. *Not Kimberly!* I really did a good job of keeping it hidden from them.

Oh my God! I especially remember one of my goddaughter's reactions once she found out. She was just fourteen at the time. I didn't want anyone to tell my family, because I wanted to be the one to tell them. Unfortunately, the media beat me to it. I was humiliated; even those closest to me didn't know. Most of them were upset by the situation, including my mom, but not my fourteen-year-old goddaughter. Honey, Simone was ecstatic. She was so happy about it and wasn't concerned about me getting in trouble. She seemed more impressed with finding out that her godmother was the Butt Lady. I can remember our conversation in detail.

The first thing out of her mouth was, "OMG, Auntie Kim, did you do Beyoncé's butt?"

"No! Girl, calm down," I said, hoping she wouldn't ask anything else about it. Beyoncé is her favorite artist, so the thought of that possibility just intrigued her.

"Okay, okay," Simone said. "But Auntie, I ain't never had no butt, and now you can give me one!" She sounded all excited.

"Baby girl, the last thing you need to be worried about is your behind. You're such a pretty young lady. You should be happy with what you have."

"But Auntie Kim, I've always wanted a butt. I see all the girls in the videos, and they all have nice butts. What's wrong with me getting one?"

"First of all, real dancers don't have big butts, and that camera is adding about ten pounds." I wanted to discourage her.

"But Auntie, I . . ."

That conversation went on for a while. We went back and forth for at least thirty minutes about the whole butt thing. Lawd, I was really having double standards at that moment. I didn't know what to do or say without sounding hypocritical.

My goddaughter loves to dance and is truly very good at it. She can also choreograph very well. She'll dance around the house, strutting in her dance attire, and I can remember looking at her and actually thinking, *My baby don't have no booty. Bless her heart.*

She even went as far as trying to make me promise that I would give her a butt when she turned twenty-one. I told her that maybe if she wanted one, she could go to a cosmetic surgeon and see what they could do for her. But by no means was she going to some black market, underground person to do it.

"But why can't you do it for me, auntie?" she asked.

I tried my best to explain I wasn't qualified to be doing those injections in the first place. I wasn't a medical professional or licensed to be doing any of that. Boy oh boy, did she give me a headache that day. She also gave me a lot to think about. Talk about double standards.

Often, I'd wonder if she wanted it done and was a grown woman, but didn't have enough fat to get a Brazilian Butt Lift, would I do it for her? Sometimes it makes me wonder because I've never had it hit so close to home. I have friends who have had it done, and they are perfectly fine. That's what I thought about, because I wanted her to be happy. But in reality, that was irrational thinking.

Sometimes it's hard to motivate people if they don't feel good about themselves or their desires aren't met. I know because I experienced it. My challenge was going to be making my goddaughter see the beauty in herself with or without a big booty. Is that even possible in today's society? With all the pressure today, will she be able to love herself correctly without it? It's a serious question, and as a culture, we really need to think about the effect this is having on young people.

Our sense of importance in the world can sometimes be attached to our physical appearance. I didn't want my goddaughter to feel as though she was less in any way simply because she didn't have a certain type of butt. We are all beautiful, but as women we need to lift each other up more and help our sisters remember that they have plenty of beauty. We must promote self-security. Not everything has to be on the competitive plane.

If you see someone, compliment them on their hair, their dress, their shoes, their body. Yes, we should all have high self-esteem, but we can help others who are lacking self-esteem by acknowledging them for their individual qualities too. That's why I have never been one to withhold compliments. If a person is due that, especially a woman, I give it to her. I compliment anything. Hair, clothes, smile, it doesn't matter.

Although I was utterly exposed, and I do mean put on front street (And honey, I thought I was going to lose my mind), in reality, the arrest helped me. I was in the rat race, and now I'm on the outside of my situation looking in because I was forced to slow down. I am a different woman now, thanks to my ability to introspect.

Today, I can look at my goddaughter and be honest with her. I can tell her what I've learned, what I've seen, and what I have been through. I can wrap it all up into one word . . . Extremities. When you put your health second and your vanity first, you are an extremist whether you want to believe that or not.

So many people have now had their butts enlarged. One of the things that made big butts so coveted was that not everybody had one. The more rare something is, the more valuable it becomes. Soon, everybody is going to have a big ol' butt. Then, I'm sure there will be something else. What will be next?

Chapter 35

Can a Sista Breathe?

The day I self-surrendered, (the courts had given me a date to report to prison to start my time) was one of the hardest things I've ever had to do. I couldn't believe it had come to this. All kinds of emotions were running through me.

First, I was sad. I was sad to leave my children and loved ones. I was angry. Anxious. A little depressed. But I must say, I was also relieved—relieved that I was going to be able to put this behind me and go on with my life.

All the things in my mind that I imagined prison would be like were wrong. It was nothing like I thought it would be. Honey, I was shocked to see the layout of Alderson Federal Prison Camp. It's nickname is "Camp Cupcake." I don't know if I would call it that, but it definitely wasn't bad. I'd heard stories of other places where people did time, but I must say it wasn't like what you see on television. Of course it has its problems, but they aren't the type of issues you'd expect would go on in a prison. But that's another story in and of itself.

Some of the magazine articles about my case had found their way into the prison. In other words, my reputation preceded me. People didn't know how to receive me. There was plenty of whispering going on around me.

"That's Smedley over there. The butt lady," I overheard one woman whisper to her friend.

"Oh shoot, that's the lady from that *Sister 2 Sister* article," another woman said in a low whisper. Not low enough though because I heard her.

Alderson was no novice to receiving women who had high profile or very public cases. Of course, this is where Martha Stewart did her stint as well as many others. I'm not likening myself to Martha, but the point is that I'm sure because of the media attention in her case, everyone was in a frenzy about her arrival.

I knew eventually the commotion would die down. My next focus was all about how I was going to do my time. Was I going to sulk and live in a state of regret? Or was I going to stand up straight, walk tall, and start fresh? I had to find a way to use my time wisely.

I am who I am. I've always gotten along well with people. I wasn't going to act any different just because I was in prison. When I finally relaxed and got over the initial shock of actually being an inmate, I was able to meet many different people. It was definitely a mixture. Some of the women were quite wonderful. Some were strange. Some were down right crazy, and I tried to avoid them altogether.

Sometimes people asked me the craziest questions.

"Excuse me. I am so sorry to bother you, but aren't you Kimberly Smedley?"

"Yes, I'm Kim," I said. "And you are?" She gave me her name and we continued talking.

"Well, Kim, I was wondering if I could ask you a few questions. I don't mean to pry, but it's personal, so could we walk and talk?" When she said that I thought about how Lonzi would say 'TWALK.' I agreed and we went outside to finish our conversation. We started walking around the compound and please believe the compound is huge. There is no fence or barbwire at Alderson, so you get a clear view of the surrounding area. The prison grounds cover approximately one square mile. It sits in the rolling

Alleghany Mountains of West Virginia, surrounded by greenery and historic brick cottages. The walk was calming.

"So what's up?" I asked her.

"Well . . . I read about your case. I actually think I have a friend that you worked on. Her body looks great. I just wanted to know if you could tell me something." She paused and looked around. Once the coast was clear, she lifted up her shirt and turned to show her butt.

"Girl, what in the world are you doing?" I asked, surprised by her actions.

"I really need my butt done. Do you see how flat it is? Do you think you can do anything for me while you're here?"

My goodness! This young lady was really tripping! Here we were in Federal Prison for breaking the law, and she was asking me to break the law all over again by doing the very same thing that I just got into trouble for. *Oh yeah, you really done lost yo' mind*, I thought. She was one of those people that I would definitely stay away from.

After that incident, people kept coming. They were asking me questions and trying to solicit me for business. They were even trying to come up with ideas to figure out how it could be done while incarcerated. That's when it hit me that there was a deeper issue at heart. A crisis was going on with women and low self-esteem. I now knew what my focus was going to be while I was serving my time. I would improve on my own character and self-esteem and try to help as many women as possible by sharing my story.

Strong self-esteem is something that probably everybody wants to have, but I can tell you that it is more like something we need to have. It's essential to us having a happy life. Without self-esteem, we are like people living in a semi-vegetative state, just

195

existing without the enjoyment of living. It helps us cope with life's disappointments, challenges, and changes. And yes, honey, everything changes. Self-esteem is the most important thing to our psychological well-being.

Life is such a beautiful but short thing. We should get all we can out of it. What better way is there to live life than to do it loving yourself unconditionally? We live in a culture that promotes "fitting in." How can we practice loving ourselves and having high self-esteem when what our society considers acceptable is constantly changing? It's not realistic to try to always live up to someone else's standards. One decade, big breasts are the thing. The next decade big butts are in. The decade after that, looking like a skeleton is the "it" thing. If you keep trying to keep up with fads, honey, you will definitely be a lost soul. We pay a high price for this type of living. And believe me, the consequences aren't worth it.

The world is becoming more and more of a competitive place. With healthy self-esteem, you won't find it necessary to be in that type of rat race. You become your own trendsetter. You love yourself so much, that you wouldn't put that type of stressful burden on your psyche. We all know that every single day, life in general does enough of that. Yet I see that many women have gone their entire lives with just enough self-esteem to enable their survival, but not enough for them to live as fully and as happily as they could. I saw this problem in prison, and I wanted to help. That was the moment I figured out what I had to do. What I felt I was supposed to do because I had a responsibility.

Although self-esteem is something that everybody needs, it is especially important for women. In our culture, women's self-esteem needs are not addressed how they should be and are not seen as an urgency the same way a man's is.

The Backside of the Story

Most of my closest friends are men, and I have a bird's eye view on how easy it is for them to get a woman. Actually, in these days, the women are the ones approaching the men. They are almost doing it more than the men approaching women.

These men don't even have to be physically attractive. They don't have to have smooth skin, six pack abs, or biceps. They don't have to be perfect or even close to it. Women will overlook those things. But on the other hand, a woman's physical appearance is the first thing a man will notice. He's looking at everything, honey, from breasts to feet. From booty to legs.

A man who values himself, has high self-esteem, and lets the world know it, is considered normal. He appears strong and is said to be demonstrating confidence and a healthy self-interest and self-image. However, on the flip side, when a woman displays those same values and displays confidence and high self-esteem, she gets an entirely different reaction. She is seen as being arrogant, grandiose, and often condemned as being vain. There is definitely a double standard.

Many times, the task of improving self-esteem seems overwhelming because a woman might feel that to like herself more, she may have to make herself over completely in order to become a more worthy being. That is not the case at all, because self-esteem comes from within.

How do we improve our self-esteem? People will often address the problem, but they don't always give you a clear solution, or a path to start on the road to improving it. A young girl may say, "Okay, yes, I can admit that I do have low self-esteem based on the definition. But how do I fix it?" I am no psychiatrist or psychologist, but the way I would start is by saying positive self-affirmations daily. Stand in front of the mirror and beat it into your mind how beautiful and special you are. That's right, while you're all alone, maybe in the bathroom or in your bedroom all alone, talk to yourself.

I AM BEAUTIFUL.
I LOVE MY PRECIOUS LIFE BECAUSE IT IS THE ONLY ONE I HAVE.
I LOVE MY BODY BECAUSE IT IS MY TEMPLE.
MY BEAUTY IS UNIQUE.
I AM AS VALUABLE AS ANYBODY ELSE.
I WILL HAVE THE BEST THAT LIFE HAS TO OFFER.
I AM A RADIANT BEING OF LOVE.
I WILL BELIEVE IN MYSELF EVEN IF NO ONE ELSE DOES.

Repeat it over and over. Convince yourself of these things. Nothing in life is free. Everything requires some level of work and care, or it will rust and die. That includes your self-esteem. If a woman has low self-esteem, she won't wake up the next day after she has acknowledged that fact and suddenly start feeling better about herself. Not without some effort. You have to work toward it and really believe in and know what you are saying about yourself is true. I'm telling you this because this is what I have to say to myself daily. I still struggle with some issues, and it is a choice I make daily to try to overcome them. You have to be active in your own salvation.

Oftentimes, we struggle with self-esteem because we compare ourselves to others. Realistically, it's practically *impossible* to go through life without comparing ourselves to other people. We assess information about ourselves and how we fit into the world by looking at ourselves in comparison to others. If we didn't, we wouldn't be able to make statements like: I am tall. I am smart. My breasts are big. My breasts are small, etc. Comparisons to others can be beneficial if we do it wisely. People who have traits or principles we admire, or have achieved things we want to aspire to achieve, can inspire us to reach our goals.

There is another side to that though. Comparisons should not become habitual, or our only way of seeing ourselves. We should never lose sight of who we are as individuals. Self-love is the greatest gift we can give to ourselves.

Chapter 36

A Hard Pill to Swallow

Once I sat down and really thought about my charges, I had so many mixed emotions. I was angry with everybody, especially the young lady responsible for igniting the FDA investigation. Mona betrayed me. We both partook in activities and knew the risks. We accepted them. I felt like she stabbed me in my back.

Regardless of the fact that what I was doing was wrong, Mona was a willing participant. I was thinking, *It wasn't so wrong when you were blowing up my phone and begging me to give you injections.* People are quick to pass the blame, but rarely acknowledge their own involvement.

One question that haunted me the most was why? Why did Mona do this to me? Like an unfinished puzzle, Mona is the missing piece you never find. You only know it's missing. I never got a clear understanding of what exactly happened with her, which is why it's difficult to detail certain events. At some point she called and said she had been hospitalized with pneumonia-like symptoms. Thereafter, I called and checked on her. Not once did she claim her illness was related to any injections I had done on her. That was in April.

Five months later, I was arrested for something pertaining to Mona. *Did she call the authorities or did the physician make the call?* To this day I still don't know. But let me say this: *If* she called the authorities because she was concerned about what I was doing and wanted me off the streets, sure, I would've been upset, but I would've understood. I however, don't believe this was a case of Mona simply trying to do the right thing, and I don't think she was coming from any place I found acceptable. There are other details that force me to conclude that her contact with authorities wasn't about anything positive. Boy oh boy, was that a hard pill to swallow. That's only *if* she made the call. Whether Mona made the call or the doctor will always remain a mystery. Nevertheless, here are the facts: all I did was try to help her. When she started coming to me, someone else had already messed her up. I didn't see myself as being a part of that. How likely was it, that she disclosed that information to the doctor?

I was mad at Marvin too. How dare he go against me? I was his woman. I thought we shared a special bond. The crazy thing was, I admitted my wrongdoings and was ready to face the punishment. If I had gone to trial and Marvin testified against me, yes that would have been messed up. What he did, however, was worse than that. He could have said, "She already pled guilty. You have her in your custody, and she's going to prison, but I won't have a hand in helping the system throw the book at her."

Marvin could have said that, but instead he testified at my sentencing. To me, that was the ultimate betrayal; it was like kicking me when I was already down. Like, "Yes, give her as much time as you can." I didn't care or think about his reasons for doing so; all I knew was that it really hurt. I thought I would never be able to forgive him.

As time went on, I started to remove myself from the selfish realm of the whole situation. It wasn't all about me. I thought about what each of them (Mona and Marvin) had to go through. This tragic event had affected them as well and had a negative impact on both of their lives. Mona was scarred emotionally and Marvin was facing criminal charges. I personalized the incidents, but in reality, they both were affected on a serious level.

The young woman's health was definitely something I was concerned about. Even though she came to me already messed up, I should have never tried to "fix" her. If I'm going to be completely honest with myself, the truth is, I wasn't qualified to be doing any of those procedures in the first place. I simply shouldn't have been doing it, and I was wrong.

I can only imagine her mindset and the feeling of wanting to lash out or get back at the black market procedures that messed her up. It wasn't all about me as an individual. There were a lot of other circumstances swirling around in the mix.

In essence, I was optimistic about not getting caught. That in itself was unrealistic and wrong as well. After all, I was so easily accessible because my full name was out there and all over the Internet. It would have been very easy to locate me, and I'm lucky to have not gotten caught up a long time ago.

After thinking about all of that, I made the decision to forgive and move on. Was that a difficult decision? Yes it was, but it was necessary. Believe me, I tried to hold on to the resentment, especially when it came to Marvin, but I couldn't. I believe the grudge I was holding started to affect my mental and physical health. The resentment, especially, was weighing down on me.

At night when I tried to go to sleep, I couldn't. My mind was running a million miles an hour. I became restless and an insomniac. It felt like there was a heavy weight on me. Almost like a brick had been placed on my chest, and it was hard to breathe. I couldn't understand what was wrong; I couldn't catch my breath. So I propped up pillows and had to sleep sitting up. It was horrible.

Finally, I said, "I need help." The kind of help that only God could give me. So I prayed. All I wanted was a decent night's sleep. I vividly remember saying, "God, I can't do this alone. I am so

202

tired. I need you to take away all the resentment and hurt I feel." I asked him to help me forgive Marvin and the victim of my crime. I felt so good saying that. Tears came to my eyes.

After praying, I remember lying back down and getting the best night's sleep that I had gotten in a long time. Honey, I slept so good that when I woke up the next morning, the pillow was on the floor. "Dang I slept good," I said quietly.

A quiet voice whispered, "That's because you let go of that heaviness that was on your chest." There is nothing like inner peace. My body was thanking me for freeing it from that thousand pound grudge I held. I was happy and relieved.

Later, I picked up a book about not forgiving and it talked about the things that happen to you when you hold on to things. It said that when you aren't willing to forgive someone, the person we refuse to forgive holds us captive. It made a lot of sense. What does a guard have to do to hold a prisoner? They have to stand there as well as watch their hostage. Both are really in the same predicament. Both can't move because the other is requiring their presence in order for imprisonment to work. That is the captor's job, their main priority, to watch the captive. I realized that was not a job I wanted to have. I wanted to be free to do the things that I have been called to do. If I could let my anger go, then it would let me go.

I also read that when you have acknowledged your purpose and your destiny, the Universe will conspire to make those things happen. We've released our desires into the ether and the Universe will place all the things we need right at our fingertips. We just have to awaken enough to make it happen and be appreciative enough to make the Universe want to give us more. It is selfish to waste your precious time and precious life being hateful or resentful when there is so much love to give and receive.

Many times I'd spoken out loud, saying I was tired and wanted to do something else. Opportunities were coming, the Universe was listening, but I was too afraid to venture into anything new. I was used to familiar territory and was scared to take a new path.

As ironic as it may sound, I remember experiencing a feeling of freedom when I walked into prison. It was a relief. And it's crazy, but for once in my life I had only me to be concerned about. I realized I couldn't control anything that was happening on the outside while I was on the inside. Often, I would use the excuse that I had to take care of this person and I had to take care of that person and so on and so forth. But once I came to prison and those people were without me, none of them dropped dead, starved, or went crazy. I was putting unnecessary burdens on myself, and it was feeding my criminal behavior.

Of course if I had the choice, I wouldn't have chosen prison for myself. I'm not sure what other circumstance would have caused me to change, and I'm not going to rack my brain trying to figure it out either. All I can say is that I'm trying to work on being a better mother, a better daughter, a better cousin, and friend and an overall better person.

Often, people don't have an eye-opening experience until they go to prison or something else bad happens. There is nothing wrong with that because it quiets you and forces you to reflect. But I felt that way before I came to prison. I started accepting that I made some wrong decisions and needed to change my life before I ever stepped foot on federal grounds. Prison just made me do it in a more pronounced way because I had so much more free time to think and reflect. It was a time to get in tune with myself. A time to plan and think about the next phase of my life.

I was no longer going to be pushed by money, friends, and family. That was a pressure I no longer allowed to be placed on myself. So many people had become dependent on me, including my two adult sons. Because of this experience, I have watched them mature into self-sufficient men. They have taken giant steps to independence and maturity. Yes, I raised them to do the right thing, but in so many ways I sheltered them from some of the real hardships of life. I didn't want them to feel all of the blows, but in reality that was a handicap. Keron was also still in therapy and had stopped self–inflicting. She was progressing well.

My children never wanted for anything. Now they were forced to see what life really was like. If I had been forced to take a time out and sit still, I don't know where I would be or what I would be doing. Who knows, maybe I'd even be dead. I was a victim of robbery a few times. Maybe I could have killed someone. I could have been doing an injection and something could have gone terribly wrong. God knows I would never have recovered from something like that. I thought about my kids having kids. What would their kids say about their grandma? What would be my legacy? All these things became a highlighted thought for me.

I finally did the most important thing I needed to do. Let it all go. I acknowledged that I am human, and sometimes we don't always have the best judgment. I vowed to not feel guilty and to use this as a stepping-stone to catapult myself to the next level. As I closed my eyes, I reflected and forgave myself. I was finally free.

Be Confident in Your Skin
by Kari Lattimore

The imperfections others may see are beauty defined.
An image of charm and grandeur and the color of strength and
survival intertwined as a portrait taken of heaven's delight.
You are beauty, you are inconceivable,
Mind-blowing, a scenic of uniqueness
And the qualities of pleasure which one can view harmoniously.
You are a queen that reigns above the elite.
You are the nature of love
Standing beyond compare like no other,
you are the brown eyes of life.
Your courage speaks life and you are fearless of the unknown.
You are the backbone of the family, yet your grace sings a
melody of peace and serenity.
You are a real woman.

You know what defines you.
You believe in what keeps you.
You stand strong with poise and self-assurance,
with the look that says you know who you are
So, be confident in your skin . . .
You are beautiful . . .
In the eyes of love you are colorless, you are shapeless
Yet you are recognized as extraordinary, distinguished.
Your charisma is genuine and magnetic.
Your love and strength releases life into the lifeless.
For in trials you keep moving steadfast and though at times you may
cry, you still find ways to look lovely at all times.
You are a real woman
With a smile that says . . . I am who I am
Always believing in yourself and knowing that
your true beauty is born from within.
So be confident in your skin . . . O beautiful woman . . .
Be confident in your own skin . . .

References

1. Singh, Devendra & Young, Robert K. (1995). Body weight, waist-to-hip ratio, breasts, and hips: Role in judgments of female attractiveness and desirability for relationships. *Ethology and Sociobiology*, 16(6), 483-507. Retrieved from http://web.missouri.edu/~rouderj/3010/readings/Singh.pdf

2. Cooper, Wilbert L. (2014). *Buttloads of pain: Illegal ass enhancements may be America's next health epidemic.* Retrieved from http://m.vice.com/read/buttloads-of-pain-0000190-v21n1

3. Du Plessis, Reverend Professor Johannes B.A., B.D. (1917). Report of the South African association for the advancement of science. *Origin and meaning of the name Hottentot.* p189-193. Retrieved from http://www.archive.org/stream/southafricanjour14sout#page/188/mode/2up

4. National Geographic Digital Motion Education Video. (2014, March 5). *Teeth Chiseling.* Retrieved from http://video.nationalgeographic.com/video/indonesia_teethchiseling

5. Beauty around the world. (2008, November 20). *O Magazine.* Retrieved from http://www.oprah.com/style/Beauty-Around-the-World/16

About the Author

Kimberly Smedley was born and raised in Atlanta, Georgia. After graduating elementary and later high school, she received her license as a cosmetologist. Her early adult life was spent working in a salon, where her main focus was enhancing the beauty of her clients. As her client base began to grow, so did her desire to shop. Once a fellow-employee noticed her careless spending habits, he advised she save her money and invest it. Using this counsel wisely, Kimberly began dabbling in real estate and excelled in the field. Eventually, she expanded into home construction until the housing market crash, ending a very prosperous run.

A trivial conversation that Kimberly engaged in with a salon regular eventually blossomed into a close brother-sister type bond. Her dearest friend/brother would be the person who would ultimately change her life in ways unimaginable. Through him, Kimberly was introduced to the underground world of silicone injections.

Years later, Kimberly's confidant passed away, and she inherited the bulk of his clientele and learned to perfect the skill. After some time, the demand for her services exploded exponentially, those new clients giving her the moniker "Miss Kim." From then on, Kimberly began transforming the backsides of everyday housewives, blue and white collar workers, celebrities, strippers, transvestites, and even the very rich.

This black market secret was well-kept for many years until 2011, when it all came tumbling down, and she was convicted of conspiracy to commit interstate commerce of a mislabeled, misbranded device.

Nevertheless, Kimberly is determined to turn her mistakes into a triumphant story, and she intends to share her experiences in hopes of educating the masses on the importance of valuing one's self-esteem, self-love, and body image.

As with most people, there are layers to Kimberly Smedley. One of her favorite hobbies is traveling the globe. She strongly believes that one of God's great creations, planet Earth, was made for us to both see and experience fully. She also has a deep appreciation for art. Helping the less fortunate and being able to make a difference in their lives one person at a time is Kimberly's true passion. She is inspired by those who are willing to pursue their dreams and refuse to accept "no" as an answer in spite of life's setbacks. She believes that *"When you stop dreaming, you stop living."*

To date, Kimberly lives in Atlanta with her three children and wants to pursue her dream of becoming a life coach and creating an all-natural skincare line. Her book, *The Backside of the Story: My Personal Journey into the Black Market Butt Injection Scandal*, is her intimate revelation of events as they occurred, which led up to her very high profile case. Creating the perfect backside is only a small facet of her former life; therefore, bigger and better aspirations await Kimberly Smedley's future.

Discussion Questions

1. What is the central idea or theme of the book?

2. Was the author successful at bringing to light the world of underground butt injections? Did the author cover the topic fairly and without bias?

3. Did any of the facts the author presented surprise you?

4. How much of a role do you believe the media plays in presenting images to the public?

5. How important are self-esteem and self-image to you?

6. Do you empathize with the author? Why or why not?

7. Was there a specific chapter that left an impression on you? Please explain.

8. What have you learned after reading this book?

9. Did this book affect you in a positive or negative way? Please explain.

10. Did you enjoy reading this book? Explain your answer.

DISCARD/SOLD
FRIENDS MLS

9 780692 224